PRODUCE TRAFFIC & TRAINS

Jeff Wilson

KALMBACH BOOKS
WAUKESHA, WI

Kalmbach Books
21027 Crossroads Circle
Waukesha, Wisconsin 53186
www.KalmbachHobbyStore.com

Published in 2018
22 21 20 19 18   1 2 3 4 5

Manufactured in China

ISBN: 978-1-62700-504-3
EISBN: 978-1-62700-505-0

Editor: Randy Rehberg
Book Design: Tom Ford

On the cover: A local ice dealer with a hoist truck tops off the bunkers of a
produce-loaded refrigerator car in Ohio in 1964. *J. David Ingles collection*

Library of Congress Control Number: 2017941412

Contents

Workers load an ice-bunker refrigerator car with wooden crates of California cherries in the 1940s. The fans on the bulkhead (top left) force cool air from the ice bunker over the load when the car is in motion. Wood strips are tacked to the crates to keep them from shifting in transit. *Southern Pacific*

INTRODUCTION

Railroads were a key force in making fresh fruits and vegetables available to almost everyone at reasonable prices throughout the country. Perishables, carried in fleets of ice-bunker refrigerator cars, represented a significant share of railroad business from the 1890s through the 1960s, with solid trains of refrigerator cars operating on priority schedules.

Unlike a load of lumber, a load of fresh fruit could go bad after even a day or two of delay. Railroad operations focused on ensuring that cars made their connections and that crews kept them iced so that their contents didn't spoil before arrival. This required frequent re-icing, accomplished at hundreds of icing platforms on railroads across the United States.

The perishable business offers many opportunities for modeling. You can model the refrigerator cars, traffic, and perishable trains regardless of the railroad or region you model, as cars traveled from growing areas to virtually every city in the country.

You can model signature elements such as fields, citrus groves, and packing houses, and even model the loading operations for various types of produce. Originating locations offer myriad operating opportunities, as switchers and locals drop off empties and pick up loads from packing houses, move cars for icing, and assemble them into trains for distant destinations.

You can also re-create the destination terminals for the loaded refrigerator cars. This ranges from the huge team-track yards of major cities such as New York and Chicago, where hundreds of cars arrived each day, to the wholesalers or food companies in large and small cities that received one or several cars at a time.

Simply modeling the traffic passing through your model railroad allows

having trains on priority schedules, possibly setting out cars or blocks of cars for local delivery or interchange connections, or perhaps stopping at an icing dock to replenish cars' ice supplies.

Focus on traditional traffic

This book focuses on the businesses, operations, and rolling stock that handled fresh fruits and vegetables.

The business began to change in the 1950s with the growth of frozen foods carried by mechanical refrigerator cars and the loss of most refrigerated traffic to trucks. Although, as chapter 7 explains, some produce traffic still travels by rail, the business is only a tiny portion of what it once was. This book centers on the operations and equipment of the "glory days" of perishable traffic and trains, mainly the 1920s through the 1960s.

We'll start with a look at the history of perishable traffic on railroads.

1

History of railroads and the produce industry

Through the mid-1800s, most fresh fruits and vegetables in the United States were grown for local consumption. There was no way to transport these perishable items long distances before they spoiled. The development of the ice-bunker refrigerator car soon allowed virtually any kind of fresh fruit or vegetable to be brought to market throughout the country, **1**.

A Santa Fe 4-8-4 powers a long string of new Santa Fe Refrigerator Department reefers near Winslow, Ariz., in the mid-1940s. This staged publicity photo highlights the importance railroads placed on perishable traffic of that era, especially for western railroads. *Santa Fe*

This early 36-foot Wickes Patent refrigerator car was built around 1900. A predecessor to more-modern ice cars, it carries lettering for the Earl Fruit Co. in California. *Milwaukee Road*

Beginnings

Perishable traffic became a significant traffic source for railroads in the last decade of the 19th century. California, which would become the country's largest producer of fruits and vegetables, was shifting from large ranching and traditional farming (harvesting grain) to smaller "truck farming" operations producing various vegetables and deciduous fruits. These operations increased in scale as growers realized that they had buyers not only locally but potentially nationally thanks to the country's expanding railroad network.

The key was the refrigerator car (or reefer). The ice-bunker reefer had been around since the 1860s but had evolved substantially by the 1890s, 2. The car had already revolutionized the meat industry and now would expand markets for fruit and vegetable growers as well. Reliable refrigerated transport meant it was now possible to ship perishable items anywhere in the country for mass consumption.

The U.S. population at the time was concentrated in the East, but most fruits and vegetables were grown in the West, Southwest, and South. This meant perishable traffic primarily represented eastbound loads to population centers—namely Chicago, New York, Philadelphia, Boston, and other large eastern cities.

In 1880, most of the 1,300 refrigerator cars in service carried products of meat packers. Refrigerator car traffic carrying meat was a fascinating business in itself, and is covered in a separate book (*Livestock & Meatpacking*, Kalmbach 2012). However, by 1890, the number of reefers had jumped to 23,000, and by 1900, 68,500 refrigerator cars were on American rails, the majority carrying fresh produce.

Produce traffic had increased dramatically. The Santa Fe in 1890 carried 3,000 carloads, but by 1900, this increased to 12,000 carloads and by 1910, 35,000 carloads. Western railroads were moving solid trains of refrigerator cars to Chicago by 1890, and in March 1888, a car of oranges traveled from Riverside, Calif., to New York City in 12 days, a record at the time.

Slow train speeds were a challenge, as were poorly insulated cars. The combination required many en route icing stations, and although many cars carried their goods without problems, far too many cars experienced spoilage and loss of contents.

Car ownership

Railroads have always been reluctant to invest in specialized equipment such as refrigerator cars (tank cars and stock cars are other examples). The reason is

3 Pacific Fruit Express was co-owned by Union Pacific and Southern Pacific. This 40-foot class R-30-12 car, built in 1923, had a wood body and steel underframe. It was typical of "modern" cars through the 1930s. *Standard Steel Car Co.*

4 Many harvests were labor intensive through the 1940s, relying heavily on migrant workers, and the potato harvest was the largest carried by railroads. Here, California workers bag potatoes in the field in the late 1940s. *Santa Fe*

5

Workers load wooden crates of citrus fruit into refrigerator cars at a packing house complex in Fort Pierce, Fla., in January 1937.
Arthur Rothstein, Library of Congress

that, unlike a boxcar, a reefer will only run loaded half the time. Refrigerator cars would also be idle in non-harvest times. As chapters 2 and 3 explain, this resulted in most refrigerator cars being owned by private owners or leasing companies—not railroads.

Railroads either contracted with a company to provide refrigerator cars or formed their own subsidiary companies to provide cars and "protective services"—the icing, ventilation, and heating that keeps cars at the proper temperatures.

The largest of these car owners was Pacific Fruit Express, which was formed in 1906 by Southern Pacific and Union Pacific, **3**. The company eventually owned 40,000 cars. The other major western railroad, the

Atchison, Topeka & Santa Fe, formed its own subsidiary company, Santa Fe Refrigerator Despatch (later Refrigerator Department). The SFRD owned more than 18,000 cars by 1930.

In the Southeast, covering substantial Florida citrus and vegetable traffic as well as other products across many states, the largest car owner was Fruit Growers Express. This company was eventually owned by more than 20 railroads, including the Atlantic Coast Line, Seaboard Air Line, Southern, and Pennsylvania.

American Refrigerator Transit owned 13,000 cars by 1940. Owned by Missouri Pacific and Wabash, ART carried a lot of traffic out of the fertile Rio Grande Valley area of Texas as well as many other central and midwestern markets.

In the Northeast, Merchants Despatch Transportation was controlled by New York Central but provided cars and services to many other railroads. Union Refrigerator Transit leased cars to many midwestern lines, including Rock Island, Minneapolis & St. Louis, Milwaukee Road, and Soo Line.

Some type of fruit or vegetable is always being harvested in the United States, and although some harvest seasons are long, some are quite short, **4**. This means a great number of cars are needed in one location for a short time. Spreading car ownership across multiple railroads allowed better use of cars and improved utilization by continually floating to the next area and crop being harvested.

Chicago and other large cities had produce yards and team tracks where dozens or hundreds of cars would arrive each day for auction and sale to local buyers. *Chicago & North Western*

Golden years

Perishable carloadings continued to increase as the country's population grew. Farms and orchards in California, Florida, Texas, Arizona, and other regions increased acreage and became more efficient with increased mechanization, better use of fertilizers, and improved plant varieties. Through the 1930s and into the mid-1940s, the railroads' share of the perishable market remained strong.

Refrigerator car design continued to improve, with better insulation materials and construction. Improved car design, including internal air-circulating fans, side wall flues, and better hatch, door, and plug designs, made more efficient use of ice and helped limit damage claims.

Train speeds also increased. Western railroads were delivering cars from California to Chicago in 6 or 7 days by the 1930s and 4 or 5 days by the 1950s, with delivery to New York in 9 or 10 days. Solid trains of refrigerator cars were common, and they operated on expedited schedules.

Railroads tightly coordinated their schedules, anticipating harvest seasons to get large fleets of cars where they were needed in time for various harvest "rushes." Frequent switching movements at packing houses and other loading areas ensured that loaded cars were quickly assembled into trains and sent on their way, **5**.

Many cars were bound for sale to produce wholesalers, grocery chains, and food processors. Others headed

to huge produce markets where their contents were auctioned and then purchased by a variety of customers, **6**. These markets were tightly coordinated with train arrivals and switching operations designed to have inbound loads ready for inspection and auctions on the mornings of market days.

A new market developed in the 1930s with the growth of frozen foods, including vegetables as well as meat, fish, and poultry. This frozen food market grew dramatically into the 1950s, with the addition of frozen concentrated juices and frozen potato products.

To handle this traffic, railroads developed "super-insulated" ice-bunker cars that—by adding 30 percent salt to the ice—could drop the internal

Mechanical refrigerator cars were developed for carrying frozen foods. They began carrying a great deal of produce by the late 1960s. This Santa Fe RR-65 car was built in 1960. *Santa Fe*

car temperature below zero. When this proved unsatisfactory, railroads began experiments in mechanical refrigeration, buying these cars in growing numbers in the 1950s, **7**.

The growth in frozen and processed foods (such as canned juices and fruits), however, meant fewer fresh perishables were being shipped. Railroads' main competition, trucks, were making a significant dent in traffic for both fresh and processed foods.

Demise of perishable traffic

Tractor-trailers with mechanical refrigeration units became common by the late 1940s, and coupled with increasing trailer sizes and improved highways, trucks began taking an ever-increasing portion of perishable traffic.

Trucks offered many advantages to shippers, mainly speed—trucks could shave days off long-distance hauls, a critical factor for many items with a short shelf life. For example, by the late 1950s, trucks had taken most strawberry traffic from the railroads—a product that once traveled in hundreds of express reefers every season.

Another key was that, although truck rates (as with railroad freight rates) were tightly regulated, there was an exception for trucks carrying agricultural products. Many trucks were already hauling finished products westward, so they were looking for eastbound backhauls anyway—cutting

rates and taking a produce load kept them moving and helped their bottom line. This was especially true for independent truckers.

Ice-bunker reefers were aging and represented old technology, especially with the many new mechanical refrigerator cars entering service. However, even though mechanical reefers had proven their reliability with frozen foods, car owners couldn't justify the additional expense for mechanical cars for produce shipments. A new mechanical car in the mid-1950s cost about $18,000, compared to $10,000 for an ice-bunker car, but their mileage earnings remained the same.

Insulated boxcars began appearing in large numbers by the late 1950s

The cost of maintaining icing stations, like this one on the Santa Fe, together with the drop in perishable traffic, contributed to the demise of the ice-bunker refrigerator car. *Santa Fe*

(see photo 26 on page 25). The advent of polystyrene and then polyurethane foam insulation and plug doors gave these cars better insulating quality than ice-bunker cars. The insulated cars were roomier and became preferred for hauling beverages and canned goods, products that ice-bunker cars had been carrying when not hauling refrigerated goods.

Reefer carloadings peaked in the late 1940s and then began trending downward. Pacific Fruit Express carried 460,000 loads in 1946 (and FGE 340,000 in the East). However, PFE's annual loads dropped to 400,000 in the early 1950s, just over 300,000 by

1960, and just over 200,000 by 1970. By the mid-1960s, railroads hauled just a third of intercity perishable traffic; by the late 1970s, this had dropped to 10 percent. Most reefer shipments that remained were for frozen goods, not fresh produce.

Ice-bunker cars dropped in number through the 1960s, and maintaining the extensive system of icing stations for a diminishing car fleet and fewer traffic movements was becoming economically unfeasible, **8**. Railroads and operators began taking icing stations out of service, and the final operator, PFE, closed its last dock in 1973.

By the 1980s, no new refrigerator cars had been built for more than 10 years. Reefer ownership was at an all-time low, and many thought that the end was near for rail perishable transport. The last two decades have seen a bit of a resurgence, however. Trinity has built new cars for Union Pacific and BNSF, and UP has rebuilt many older cars (see chapter 2). Loads of frozen products and perishables are still traveling from coast to coast, albeit nowhere near the numbers of the mid-1900s.

Next, we'll take a look at how refrigerator cars developed and how they evolved from ice-bunker cars to high-tech mechanical and cryogenic cars.

CHAPTER TWO

Refrigerator cars

A Pacific Fruit Express mechanical car stands out among Santa Fe and PFE 40-foot ice-bunker cars in this early 1960s train. Mechanical cars were developed for frozen goods but began hauling more fresh produce by the 1960s, eventually pushing ice cars out of service in the 1970s. *J. David Ingles collection*

The ice-bunker refrigerator car was the primary method of hauling perishables from the 1800s through the heyday of fruit and vegetable transport by rail. Ice reefers evolved significantly through the 1950s, with mechanical cars taking over from the 1960s through today, **1**.

California Fruit Express was an 1890s private car operator. This all-wood Wickes Patent car, built in 1892, was 36 feet long with a 30-ton capacity and held 7,500 pounds of ice. *Trains magazine collection*

Although the idea for an ice-cooled car was no longer novel by the late 1800s, railroads of the period were reluctant to invest money in them. Railroads had substantial fleets of boxcars and did not want to invest in rolling stock designed for specialty commodities.

Not only were refrigerator cars more expensive to build than boxcars, they required extensive icing stations and ice supplies to keep them cold. They would spend half of their service lives running empty, returning to their owners, and since perishable traffic was seasonal, cars would sit idle for extended periods each year. In addition, perishable traffic spoiled easily, required constant care, and resulted in higher and more frequent damage claims than other freight.

The result was that private owners and leasing companies soon became the largest owners of refrigerator cars. By 1900, almost 80 percent of reefers in service (54,000 of 68,500) were privately owned. The largest early private owner was Armour, the meatpacking giant. At the turn of the 20th century, Armour owned about

20,000 cars, the majority of which were actually leased to carry perishable traffic (mainly from the West). The company also owned icing stations throughout the country.

Railroads soon found the way to acquire refrigerator cars was to form separate subsidiary companies to own and manage them (more on this in chapter 3). In 1906, Pacific Fruit Express was formed, co-owned by the Union Pacific and Southern Pacific. Other major refrigerator car owners included American Refrigerator Transit, Burlington Refrigerator Express, Fruit Growers Express, Merchants Despatch Transportation, Northern Refrigerator Line, Santa Fe Refrigerator Department, Union Refrigerator Transit, and Western Fruit Express.

Early construction

Although ice-cooled cars—converted boxcars with insulated walls and ice chests—were first used in the 1850s and 1860s, the first patent for a refrigerator car was awarded to J. B. Sutherland in 1867. His design called for ice tanks inside each end

of a car, with vents above the tanks providing air circulation to the interior. The basic design—with modifications and upgrades—would last through the end of the ice-bunker era.

A number of companies and individuals began building cars, and among the most common early cars were the Tiffany Patent and Wickes Patent cars, **2**. The Tiffany car had an overhead ice bunker running the length of the car. The Wickes car was more conventional, with ice bunkers at each end and overhead hatches at each corner (two per bunker) for adding ice. Variations of this design became popular. As cars proved themselves capable of carrying perishables long distances, reefer ownership grew dramatically: from 6,000 cars in 1885 to 23,000 by 1890 and 68,000 in 1900.

At the turn of the 20th century a typical refrigerator car was 32–36 feet long, with all-wood construction, a truss-rod underframe, and archbar trucks, **3**. Car capacity ranged from 20–30 tons, with a light weight around 37,000 pounds and an ice bunker capacity of about 7,000 pounds.

3

This 38-foot wood Duluth, Missabe & Iron Range car, built in 1910, has a steel center sill, truss rods, and archbar trucks. The 25-ton car was still in on-line service in the early 1960s. *J. David Ingles collection*

4

In the 1920s, American Car & Foundry built thousands of refrigerator cars based on the USRA design with a fishbelly underframe, including American Refrigerator Transit 22677, shown here in 1948. *Mainline Photos*

5

Union Refrigerator Transit no. 8009, built in 1931, at first resembles the ART AC&F reefer. However, it has a conventional underframe, lacks the exposed side sills and corner reinforcing angles of the ART car, and has a wood fascia strip along the top of the side instead of a metal angle. *J. David Ingles collection*

The basic car superstructure followed contemporary boxcar design, with double-sheathed (double-wall) construction and insulation between the walls. Insulation was a major source of trouble with early cars. Loose materials, such as cattle hair and sawdust, were poor insulators to start with, and as cars aged, the material settled, leaving large areas in the walls without insulation. If moisture leaked into the insulation space, materials would clump and lose insulating qualities, compounding the problem.

Improvements by the start of the 1900s included blankets of felted hair or flax fiber nailed between walls, which—although far from ideal—stayed in place.

Hatches followed several designs. They were hinged doors secured by latch bars, with insulating plugs on the inside that fit snugly in the bunker opening. Most cars in fruit and vegetable service from the 1920s onward could be operated in ventilator service. For this, the latches had notches that allowed the hatches to be propped open at an angle. When the train was in motion, this circulated air through the car.

Produce cars had ice bunkers made of wire or mesh that held chunk ice and allowed air circulation and drainage of melted ice. This water drained from the bunkers through a pipe or spout at each corner of the car.

Some cars had brine tanks instead of conventional bunkers. These were primarily meat-service cars and not used for fruit and vegetable service. With brine tanks, a mix of crushed ice and salt was used. These cars could not be used in ventilator service.

Swinging doors originally had simple latch hooks, which weren't reliable for keeping doors closed tightly. In the early 1900s, Miner first offered what became the standard design, with a vertical latch bar (on the right-side door, with a handle to the left) that locked securely in hasps above and below the door opening. Each door was 2 feet wide, with a 4-foot-wide opening (except for Santa Fe, which used 5-foot-wide openings).

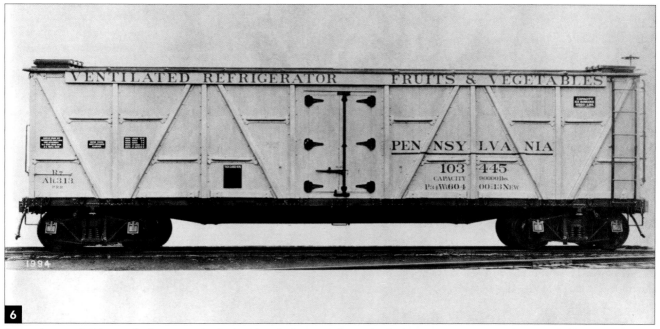

Pennsylvania's R7 design, built in 1913, had a steel underframe and steel body framing. It was unusual for its single-sheathed (exposed bracing) design. *Pennsylvania Railroad*

Slatted floor racks were another early 1900s development, allowing much better cold air circulation throughout the car compared to solid floors.

Wood car development

Steel center sills had become common for freight cars by the turn of the century. By the late 1910s, steel underframes were standard, even though body construction for reefers was still wood.

The comparatively few buyers for reefers (compared to hundreds of railroads buying boxcars) meant car designs were often specific to certain builders or owners. It's pretty easy, for example, to identify many classes of Pacific Fruit Express or Santa Fe cars by spotting features.

The United States Railroad Administration (USRA) developed several standard freight car designs during its period of control of U.S. railroads during World War I. Although a refrigerator car was among the designs—a 40-foot, wood-body car with deep steel (fishbelly) underframe—none were built under USRA control.

American Car & Foundry built thousands of wood cars from the 1910s into the 1930s similar to the USRA design, with fishbelly underframes and straight side sills, **4**. Major owners included American Refrigerator Transit, Union Refrigerator Transit, and Western Refrigerator Lines.

Modelers and railfans have divided the AC&F cars into groups: built **1911–1915** (type 1) with deep (30") fishbellies and short doors, **1915–1926** (type 2) with taller doors and upgraded hardware and roof hatches, and **1926–1931** (type 3) with shallower (24") fishbelly center sills. Many of the later cars survived into the 1950s, and some were rebuilt and lasted through the 1960s.

General American was another prolific builder of wood refrigerator cars, turning out thousands of similar cars during that period. They look at first glance like AC&F cars, but they lack the fishbelly underframes, **5**.

Pacific Fruit Express (photo 3 on page 7) and Santa Fe Refrigerator Department (photo 6 on page 31) both had many large groups of wood cars of their own designs. More details on each are listed in chapter 3.

Steel body framing was common on boxcars by the 1920s, which improved strength and increased car life. The Pennsylvania R7 of the early teens was among the first steel-framed reefers, and it's easy to spot because of its single-sheathed construction, **6**. The Pennsy built about 3,000 of them, and as part of the Fruit Growers Express fleet, they could be seen across the country.

Insulation and bunkers made reefer interiors smaller than boxcars. A 40-foot refrigerator car interior was about 33 feet long, 8 feet wide, and 7 feet tall, compared to 9'-2" wide and 10'-0" tall for an early ARA boxcar.

All-steel boxcars were common by the 1930s, but many refrigerator cars continued to use wood (often with "outside metal roofs," which were metal sheets applied over a wood roof for insulation). The thought was that steel would transmit heat too readily, so wood was preferable for its insulating qualities.

Even after steel refrigerator cars debuted in 1936, some cars continued to be built with wood sheathing into the 1940s. Fruit Growers Express and Western Fruit Express acquired wood cars as late as 1946. Many wood cars built in the 1920s and after remained in service through the 1960s and into the 1970s—albeit rebuilt. Some were rebuilt with steel ends and roofs, but many retained wood sides and ends until retirement, **7**. In 1962, PFE still operated about 4,000 wood cars (of 22,000 total ice cars).

Soo (URTX) no. 1941 was built in 1931. It's similar to the Milwaukee car in photo 5 but, by the '60s, it was rebuilt with steel ends and roof. *J. David Ingles collection*

The first steel reefers were Pacific Fruit Express class R-40-10 cars in 1936. They had early Dreadnaught ends and tabbed side sills. *Trains magazine collection*

PFE's largest class of steel reefers was the 5,000 cars of R-40-23 starting in 1947. They had improved Dreadnaught ends, fans, and steel running boards. *Mainline Photos*

Most cars through the wood era had capacities of 30 or 40 tons, compared to 50 tons for a contemporary boxcar. Perishable loads were relatively light (between 12 and 25 tons for a typical fruit or vegetable load), and with the smaller interior, even a load of "heavy" canned goods rarely exceeded 35 tons.

The rated capacity usually wasn't a function of the body but of the trucks. Having a lighter load limit allowed a smaller spring package, which led to a smoother ride for the lighter cars, important for higher-speed service.

Car rebuilding

As refrigerator cars aged, owners considered several variables: the condition of the cars, the cost of rebuilding compared to a new car, the estimated extended lifespan of the rebuilt car, the anticipated annual maintenance costs for each, and the allowable tax deductions along with depreciation of the cars.

For freight cars, rebuilding would have to significantly extend the life of the car (generally at least 10 to 15 years, as a new steel car should last 30 to 40 years).

The Santa Fe was the leading rebuilder of refrigerator cars (see photo **14**). Instead of buying new steel cars, SFRD from 1936 to 1954 rebuilt more than 12,000 of its older wood cars with steel bodies.

PFE also rebuilt thousands of its older wood cars. Unlike SFRD, PFE cars generally kept wood sheathing on their sides but received new steel ends, roofs, and hardware. Other owners also rebuilt cars, including ART, FGE, and MDT.

The extent of rebuilding varied by owner. In many cases, cars were stripped to their framework, with new sides, ends, and roofs. New, up-to-date insulation was added. Trucks were sometimes reconditioned and in other cases replaced. Brakes were upgraded—older K brakes were replaced by AB systems and older vertical brake staffs were replaced by geared brake wheels.

Wood cars required a lot of maintenance. Wood sheathing became worn and warped by water and salt, with boards often requiring repair or replacement. It wasn't uncommon for wood cars to be repainted every 5 or 6 years, whereas steel cars could last much longer. Early wood-framed cars required complete rebuilding every 10 or 15 years, but later steel-framed wood cars of the 1920s and '30s lasted longer.

Steel cars

In the 1930s and '40s, it was the American Railway Association (ARA) and later American Association of Railroads (AAR) that developed standardized car designs—but not for refrigerator cars. Even so, manufacturers tended to follow contemporary boxcar designs when building steel reefers, especially with common components like ends, roofs, underframes, and brake gear. The sidebar on page 23 lists typical spotting features.

The first all-steel reefers were the 4,700 cars of PFE's R-40-10 class built in 1936, **8**. The R-40-10s were 40-foot cars that can be spotted by their square-corner-post 4/4 Dreadnaught ends, riveted vertical side panels, and the tabs extending below the sides to cover the ends of the bolsters and cross bearers. As built, they had wood running boards, but many were later upgraded with steel running boards and air-circulating fans.

Steel cars also appeared that year or the next in fleets of Burlington Refrigerator Express, Illinois Central, and Western Fruit Express, and for many other owners into the 1940s.

What became "the signature steel car" of the ice era is PFE's largest class of steel reefers, the 40-foot R-40-23 car, **9**. Built in 1947, the 5,000 cars epitomized the "modern" ice reefer, with air-circulating fans and convertible bunker walls that folded to the sides to increase capacity when ice refrigeration wasn't needed (or for top-ice loads), **10**.

The cars featured up-to-date construction, with improved 3/3 Dreadnaught ends with W-corner posts (giving them rounded corners compared to the square corners of

10 Collapsible bulkheads swung inward from the bunker, which increased car capacity when an ice load wasn't needed. *American Car & Foundry*

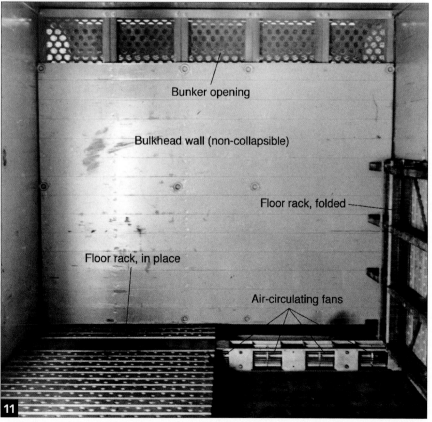

11 Early air circulation fans were at floor level under the racks. They drew air from the car and forced it upward through the bunker. *Santa Fe*

17

12 The fan generator was powered by a rubber-coated wheel in contact with the tread of a car wheel. The lever at left turned the fan on and off. *Preco*

13 Attaching a portable precooling motor (right) with a belt to the shaft extension on the generator enabled the car's own fans to precool a load while standing still. *Preco*

R-40-10 cars). The new cars were also 3" taller than the older cars.

A feature of most produce-service steel cars were air-circulating fans, which first appeared in 1941, **11**. These made ice-bunker cars more efficient by forcing cold air throughout the entire load and evening the temperature throughout. Also helping efficiency were flues built into the sides of the car that improved air circulation.

Early fans were driven directly by a rubber wheel in contact with a rail wheel tread, connected by belts and pulleys. Mechanical problems (including fires from overheated bearings) quickly led to the adaptation of electrically powered fans driven by a wheel-driven generator. A handle extending downward from the car side turned the fans on and off by moving the rubber wheel from the rail wheel, **12**. Fan-equipped cars are marked by a disk on the lower-left side of the car.

Fan cars have a mounting location for a separate precooling motor that can be attached to turn the generator while the car is stationary. Doing this allows a car's load to be precooled while standing still, **13**.

Fans were initially located at the bottoms of the bunkers, just under the floor racks. They forced air into the bottoms of the bunkers, upward through the ice so it flowed back out over the load. By the early 1950s (with PFE's R-40-26), fans were moved to the tops of the bunkers so that they blew cold air from the bunkers outward over the load, drawing air upward from the bunkers (see photo on page 4). This was more efficient and kept fans out of drainage areas under the bunkers.

Fans were used whenever a perishable shipment was being carried with ice in bunkers, except for cars in top-ice service, when fans would be off.

Another distinctive steel design first appeared in 1939. These had horizontal side sheets (instead of vertical) with the top piece overlapping the bottom, designed to reduce chances of leakage at seams. The result was a distinctive-looking car with a horizontal seam and rivets running the middle of the length of the car.

The first of these 42-foot cars were for American Refrigerator Transit, which built the first 775 using kits supplied by AC&F. These had square-corner 4/4 Dreadnaught ends. In 1947 and 1948, ART ordered (or built) almost 2,300 similar cars, but with improved Dreadnaught 3/3 ends and a later batch had straight side sills, **14**.

General American built many cars of this basic design for Union Refrigerator Transit (which was owned by General American). URTX leased them to several railroads and packing companies.

Sliding plug doors began appearing in 1950 on PFE's R-40-26 and SFRD's Rr-49 (rebuilt) cars, **15**. These cars had 6-foot-wide openings. Sliding doors would soon become standard for refrigerator cars.

Another feature appearing at that time was stage icing. Folding down a grate at the half-height level of each bunker allowed carrying a half-load of ice more efficiently than simply filling a bunker halfway.

Insulation was also continuing to improve. Fiberglass and reflective backing were common by 1952, with insulation board and blankets (such as Hairinsul and Mineral Fibre) and then Styrofoam by the late 1950s.

Demise of ice cars

As more perishable traffic moved to trucks and mechanical reefers, ice car fleets began to trend downward. Ice-bunker cars became victims of a service threshold: To provide the needed infrastructure of ice making, supplying icing platforms, the labor of icing cars, and providing cleanout or repair services, a high volume of traffic was needed. As carloads declined and larger mechanical cars came into use, the car fleet dropped below the profitable threshold and the expenses of operating ice cars increased.

By the mid-1960s, with fewer cars in service (and many of those in use reaching the ends of their lifespans), the system became untenable. Many icing platforms were taken out of service by 1970. The Santa Fe (SFRD) discontinued ice service in 1971, and PFE—the last to do so—shut down its remaining platforms in late 1973.

Most of American Refrigerator Transit's steel cars had horizontal side sheets with a seam down the middle of each side. This fan-equipped car was built in 1947. *Mainline Photos*

Santa Fe rebuilt older wood cars with steel sides instead of buying new cars. The Rr-49 class introduced sliding plug doors in 1950. *Santa Fe*

"Super-insulated" cars had thicker than standard insulation and extra ice capacity compared to other reefers for handling frozen foods. This 50-foot PFE class R-70-2 car was built in 1932. *Pacific Fruit Express*

Fruit Growers Express helped pioneer mechanical refrigerator cars. This 55-foot, 60-ton car was built in 1957 and just had a new refrigeration unit installed before this 1975 photo. *Jeff Wilson collection*

This engine and refrigeration unit is in the end of a Pacific Fruit Express R-40-30 car built in 1958. The car end is at left and the bulkhead is to the right. *Trane Corp.*

Number 460393 was one of 600 PFE R-70-25 cars built in 1971. The 57-footers were the last new PFE reefers built and among the last reefers built for 20 years. *Jim Hediger*

You could, however, still find ice-bunker cars in service through the 1970s. Some remained in top-ice vegetable (TIV) service, which used finely crushed ice sprayed atop the load at initial loading points.

Other old ice cars continued operating simply as insulated cars, with bunker bulkheads removed, hauling canned goods and beverages. Most of these cars were retired by 1980 (PFE had 3,500 in service in 1973 and 560 in 1978).

Large and super-insulated cars

Most ice-bunker freight reefers (non-express cars) were 36 to 42 feet long, but some 50-footers were built beginning in the 1930s. Most of these were so-called "super-insulated" cars designed for the frozen food industry.

Frozen foods required subzero temperatures to stay solid. The only way to do this with ice-bunker cars was to add 30 percent salt with the bunker ice. This made the ice melt faster, resulting in lower temperatures. Combined with extra insulation, this would drop the temperature to a few degrees below zero.

Santa Fe had built 100 standard 50-foot wood cars in 1931, and experimented by rebuilding 10 of them with heavy insulation in 1936. Pleased with the results, SFRD ordered 200 similar steel 50-footers from General American in 1937 and another 150 in 1940. It also rebuilt another 75 of the older 50-footers.

Pacific Fruit Express also had similar cars: 100 50-foot, 70-ton wood cars built in 1932 (class R-70-2), **16**. PFE added another 1,000 wood 50-footers into the 1940s and 187 steel 50-footers in the early 1950s. Other carriers also operated 40- or 50-foot super-insulated cars, including American Refrigerator Transit, Fruit Growers Express, Merchants Despatch, Union Refrigerator, Western Fruit Express, Burlington Refrigerator Express, North Western, and Northern Pacific.

Mechanical reefers

Mechanical cars were slow to catch on for three reasons, **17**. First, railroads

This North Western Refrigerator Line Car, built by AC&F in 1928, displays a bold billboard scheme, common to the period, that would disappear by the early 1930s. *AC&F*

Billboard reefers

From the 1910s into the 1930s, refrigerator car owners often painted cars in bright, colorful schemes with bold lettering and logos advertising a number of products, from meat to dairy and beverages.

In 1934, the Interstate Commerce Commission released a ruling on these cars that is often referred to as "banning billboard reefers," but this is really incorrect. What the ICC ruling was actually about was rebates from a car lessor to a lessee. The key part for paint schemes was that large billboard schemes amounted to an illegal rebate to a lessee. Following the ruling, no new such schemes could be applied, and in 1937 these cars could no longer accepted for interchange.

The bottom line was that reefers could not carry logos and lettering not belonging to the owner; cars leased to a single shipper could have the shipper's name and emblem but could not advertise specific products.

This didn't have much of an effect on produce cars since specific products and owners rarely applied to the market, but the topic comes up often among modelers. For a thorough discussion and hundreds of photos, see *Billboard Refrigerator Cars* by Richard Hendrickson and Edward Kaminski (Signature Press, 2008).

already had an extensive system of icing platforms in place around the country. Second, ice refrigeration—although time and labor intensive—was reliable. The third, and main reason, was that mechanical cars were significantly more expensive to build than an ice car (in the late 1950s about $20,000 for a mechanical car vs. $12,000 for an ice car).

Another issue was humidity control. Most fruits and vegetables in cold storage require humidity at 85 percent or higher, but mechanical refrigeration removes moisture from the air, lowering humidity. This can cause drying, shrinkage, and lowered quality for some produce. To combat

this, shippers developed new methods of packing and shipping products, such as wrapping products tightly (often in supermarket-ready packaging).

The initial push for mechanical cars came not from produce shippers but from the frozen food industry, which was experiencing rapid growth from its beginnings in the late 1930s. First came packaged frozen meats, fish, and vegetables and then frozen potato products and frozen concentrated orange juice (FCOJ).

Fruit Growers Express was the first to take the plunge, buying 25 mechanical cars in 1949 to tap the growing FCOJ traffic in Florida. FGE

(with partners BREX and WFEX) in 1948 began testing various types of refrigeration units, including ammonia and dry ice cars as well as diesel- and gas-powered mechanical units. The diesel versions proved the best option and became standard for mechanical reefers. Refrigeration units came from several builders, including Carrier, Frigidaire, Thermo-King, Trane, and Waukesha.

To cool the car, a small diesel engine turns an alternator that powers a compressor in the refrigeration unit. The engine and refrigeration unit are contained in a compartment at one end of the car, identifiable by an exterior

20

This 68-foot high-cube Cryo-Trans refrigerator car was built in 2000. As built, these cars were cooled with frozen carbon dioxide. They have since been rebuilt with end-mounted mechanical units. *Jeff Wilson*

21

Trinity began building TrinCool refrigerator cars in 1998. This 72-foot version belongs to UP, and Trinity also makes 64-foot versions of the high-cube car. *Jeff Wilson*

22

Great Northern 2116 is an example of a wood-body, steel-underframe express reefer. The 50-foot car has a 35-ton capacity. *Great Northern*

screened or louvered panel, **18**. Fans and ductwork carry the cold air into the car. The units provide heat as well, eliminating the need for portable charcoal and alcohol heaters used in ice-bunker cars.

These cars carry fuel tanks under the body—up to 400 gallons, often in two tanks—allowing the unit to run up to two weeks before refueling. Thermometers with exterior gauges allow checking temperatures without opening the door.

Early cooling systems were of two types: constant running, appropriate for frozen lading only, or thermostatically controlled, which allows setting the interior temperature to match the lading. Mechanical units allow subzero (to 20 below) temps.

Pacific Fruit Express and SFRD ordered mechanical cars in 1952. About 1,200 mechanical cars were in service by 1955: 600 for the FGE/BREX/WFEX consortium, 330 for PFE, and 180 for SFRD. By 1960, the total was about 5,000—significant, but still just 4 percent of the 125,000 total reefers operating.

Mechanical cars wouldn't carry fresh produce on a large scale until the late 1960s as fleets grew large enough to cover both markets. For example,

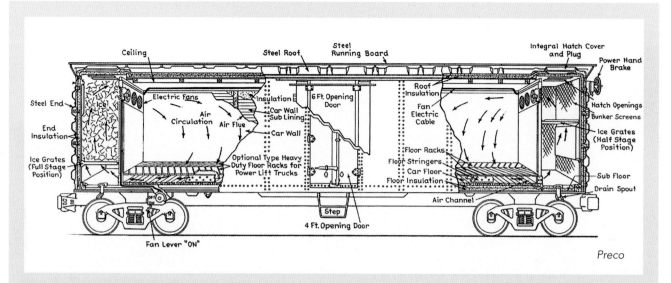

Car spotting features

Cars were built to many designs over the years, and many characteristics are unique to certain owners or builders, or to specific car types. To identify a car, start with the basic dimensions (length and height). Then look at each individual feature of the car.

Sides—Are they wood (vertical tongue-and-groove boards), plywood, or steel? For wood: Are there angled straps around the ends and/or angled straps across the corners? Is the side sill a separate piece, and is it smooth or channel-shaped?

For steel cars: How many panels are used, and are the seams vertical or horizontal? Are seams riveted or welded? Is the side sill straight, or are there tabs extending down to cover the ends of the cross bearers and bolsters?

For mechanical cars (and insulated boxcars) with vertical exterior posts: How many posts are used? What style are they? Are any posts angled? Also examine the location and size of grab irons and ladders.

Ends—Are they wood or steel? For steel: What type of end is used? Most steel ends were Dreadnaught, with square corner posts (early) or rounded W-posts (early 1940s and later), and found in a variety of corrugation arrangements: count the number of ribs on the top and bottom sections, as in 3/3 or 4/4. Improved ends have a different corrugation shape.

Doors—Are doors swinging or sliding plug? How wide and tall is the door opening? For plug: How wide is the door? How many vertical latch bars are there, and what type of release handle is used?

Roof—Many early cars had wood roofs, and some were covered with tarpaper or thin metal sheathing. These could be peaked or rounded (radial). Steel roofs followed the same styles as boxcars, with Viking and then Murphy panel roofs on early cars, followed by diagonal-panel roofs on later cars. Also look at the style of the roof hatches and running boards (wood or metal in various styles).

Underframe—Early wood cars had truss-rod underframes, easily visible from the side. Later wood (and some early steel) cars had deep steel fishbelly center sills, which are also readily visible. Most steel cars had standard underframes, and many insulated (RBL) cars and mechanical reefers had cushion underframes of various designs.

Brakes—Cars had K brakes into the 1930s, with AB brake gear required on new cars as of 1932. K brakes were banned from interchange service in 1953, so many older cars were converted to AB brakes. Check the style of brake wheel on the ends.

Trucks—Andrews and Vulcan trucks were popular through the 1920s but were banned from interchange in 1956. Ice cars continued using various types of solid-bearing trucks through the end of their service lives in the 1970s, but most mechanical cars received roller-bearing trucks when built.

---

in 1962, PFE operated about 3,000 mechanical cars (of 25,000 total cars), and almost all were in frozen food service. By 1969, however, almost half of PFE's 18,000 cars were mechanical.

Increasing capacity

A benefit of mechanical refrigeration was increased capacity. The more efficient refrigeration equipment and air circulation allowed increased length, height, and cubic capacity as well as weight. Initial mechanical cars had nominal 50-ton capacity (most steel ice cars were 30 or 40 tons), and by the late 1950s and early '60s, reefers followed the industry standard by moving to 70-ton nominal capacity cars.

Foam insulation, appearing in the 1950s, was another major improvement. Foam had a much higher insulation value in a thinner layer than earlier fiber and blanket insulations, enabling a thinner roof and walls.

Declining markets and the trend of produce and frozen goods moving to trucks meant that, even with the retirement of ice cars, railroads had plenty of capacity in existing mechanical refrigerators by the early 1970s, **19**. No new mechanical cars were built for more than 20 years after

Santa Fe rebuilt no. 4045 from an older 50-foot wood car (built by General American in 1924) with steel sides and ends in the mid-1930s. *Trains magazine collection*

Railway Express Agency no. 6285 is a modern steel express reefer. The 55-foot car is one of 500 built by American Car & Foundry in 1947 and 1948. *J. David Ingles collection*

Canadian National subsidiary Grand Trunk Western had 100 overhead-bunker refrigerator cars (having eight roof hatches) with underbody heaters built in 1955. *J. David Ingles collection*

1973, and by the early 1980s, it looked like the era of the refrigerator car might be over.

Modern reefers

Around 1990, a new style of car began appearing, cooled by cryogenics (frozen carbon dioxide) and designed for carrying frozen potato products from the Northwest. Starting in the early 1980s, several former Burlington Northern Fruit Express and Santa Fe mechanical cars were rebuilt with cryogenic refrigeration.

About 350 new cars followed, built by Gunderson starting in 1990. These cars are 68 feet long with smooth welded sides and 10-foot doors, **20**. They are excess-height cars—just under 17 feet, with an 11'-3" interior height. They were operated by Cryo-Trans and General American (ArctiCar). They could maintain below-zero temperatures for up to two weeks on a single 15-ton charge of CO_2.

These cars remain in service, but the rising price of frozen carbon dioxide led to their conversion to mechanical refrigeration with end-mounted reefer units in 2000–2001. Cryo-Trans maintains a fleet of about 1,400 mechanical cars (CRYX reporting marks).

Total refrigerator cars in service dropped to a low of around 8,000 by 2001. However, new service implemented by Union Pacific and CSX (see chapter 7) began to increase demand, and UP began rebuilding many older cars with new refrigeration units, along with GPS and temperature tracking features.

These cars included former UPFE cars as well as former FGE and Santa Fe cars. They received white paint schemes with ARMN reporting marks.

In 1998, UP bought 50 new 72-foot cars from Trinity featuring composite fiberglass bodies with end-mounted refrigeration units, **21**. This was followed by 1,500 new Trinity 64-foot cars in 2003 and an additional 225 cars from Greenbrier. They have GPS tracking with remote diagnostics and data capability.

Express reefers

Expedited shipments were carried in express refrigerator cars as head-end traffic in passenger or express trains. Through the 1940s, most express reefers featured wood construction with steel underframes, and were typically longer (50 feet) compared to standard reefers, **22**. They rode on high-speed, four-wheel trucks and were equipped with steam lines, signal lines, and passenger-type brake systems. They were classified BR (with bunkers) or BS (brine tanks) by the AAR.

Express reefers were operated by Railway Express Agency (American Railway Express before REA's formation in 1929, and individual express companies before 1917). Some cars were owned by REA, although many cars were owned by individual railroads (or subsidiary companies, such as Pacific Fruit Express) and either leased by REA or operated under REA direction. These cars were lettered for owning railroads, but many carried REA lettering as well.

In the 1920s, Pullman, General American, and American Car & Foundry built 50-foot wood cars with radial (curved) or arched roofs (canvas covered). By the late 1930s, express reefers were steel, typically with smooth sides and ends, steel roofs, and

26

Overhead-bunker cars had an ice hatch for each individual brine tank. This is a Canadian National car. *Canadian National*

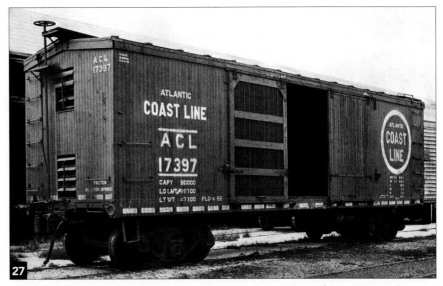

27

Ventilated boxcars were common on railroads in the Southeast for carrying melons. They had adjustable end vents and two doors: one solid and one with screens or slats. *Trains magazine collection*

Insulated boxcars became popular for beverages, canned goods, and other products requiring protection but not refrigeration. Burlington Refrigerator Express acquired this 50-foot car in 1958. *J. David Ingles collection*

swinging side doors. Many were rebuilt from older wood cars, **23**. Inside, many had collapsible bulkheads to provide more room for standard express parcels when operated in nonrefrigerated service.

By the mid-1940s, steel express cars began closely resembling contemporary AAR-design cars, albeit with high-speed trucks and steam and signal lines. Notable of these were 1,000 55-foot plug-door cars for Railway Express Agency in 1947 and 1955, **24**.

Similar cars were built for Great Northern (50, 2200–2249) in 1952 and Atlantic Coast Line, 50 cars from ACF identical to the first REA cars in 1947–48 (3000–3049). Santa Fe built 50 56-foot plug-door cars (4050–4099) in 1953.

Another group of steel express reefers were rebuilt from former World War II troop sleepers in the late 1940s, which can be spotted by their plated-over window openings on each side and their 5-foot swinging doors (see chapter 3).

Overhead-bunker cars

Cars with overhead ice bunkers were not common in the United States, but many ran on Canadian railroads and subsidiaries beginning in the late 1930s, **25**. Unlike the U.S., Canadian railroads (Canadian National and Canadian Pacific) owned the refrigerator cars used in both meat and perishable service, although in Canada, meat products were a more common load. Canadian Pacific acquired 50 overhead-bunker wood cars in 1938, which proved successful. Additional steel cars were soon purchased, with about 3,000 in service by 1950, including 100 on CN subsidiary Grand Trunk Western.

These cars used eight individual brine tanks, each with its own roof hatch, **26**. Conventional bunkers wouldn't work overhead, as the melting water would drain down on top of the load. The main advantage was efficiency: the cars had a 7,000-pound ice capacity, compared to 11,000 for a

conventional car, and were effective at providing uniform temperature across the entire car.

The Canadian cars were also equipped with underbody heaters (charcoal through the 1950s, butane after that), which heated liquid circulating in interior pipes near the walls under the floor racks.

In the United States, overhead-bunker cars were experimental, with ART, FGE, and PFE all having some cars (see photo 3 on page 100). Disadvantages were icing (crushed ice required instead of chunk), the risk of load contamination from leaking brine tanks, and—a big one for U.S. lines—the inability to use the cars in ventilator service (or the use of fans).

Ventilated boxcars

Another car that carried perishables is the ventilated boxcar, **27**. Construction details varied, but these typically had two sliding doors on each side: one solid and one with an opening covered

The Pacific Fruit Express and New York Central (owned by MDT) 40-foot trailers are both actually containers on bogies, carrying produce from California to New York. PFE also owned several piggyback flats as well. *Trains magazine collection*

by a screen, grate, or slats. The car ends had screened or slatted openings that could be covered.

This design allowed air to flow through the car in similar fashion to an ice-bunker reefer with hatches open in ventilator service. These cars were also known as "melon" or "watermelon" cars for their most-common ladings.

Ventilated cars were most popular in watermelon-growing areas of the Southeast. Major owners included Atlantic Coast Line, Seaboard Air Line, Central of Georgia, and Louisville & Nashville. They were common from the turn of the 20th century through the 1940s (more than 10,000 were in service in 1942), but most were supplanted by conventional ventilator reefers by the end of the 1950s.

Insulated boxcars

The advent of polystyrene and polyurethane foam insulation in the 1950s revolutionized insulated car design. The foam could be sprayed into gaps and would expand to fill space. Thin layers of foam were more efficient than thick layers of fiberglass or other material.

Insulated cars were ideal for perishables that didn't require temperatures near freezing, **28**. These cars were also ideal for loads requiring climate control but not cooling, such as canned goods and beverages.

Among the first were an order of 550 40-foot cars split between Bangor & Aroostook and the New Haven, built by Pacific Car & Foundry in 1953 (see photo 43 on page 49). These 40-ton, plug-door cars were mainly used for hauling potatoes and were also equipped with underbody heaters.

Fruit Growers Express followed with an order of 40-foot cars in 1954. Many other railroads and refrigerator lines soon ordered insulated cars as well. Initially given the AAR car code XL (later XI) for "insulated boxcar," subsequent cars were often classified RB (bunkerless refrigerator) or RBL

(bunkerless refrigerator with load restraints/dividers).

By the 1960s, insulated boxcars had stretched to 50 feet and longer, with 70-ton capacity (100 tons by the late 1960s). Many cars through this period featured the same construction as contemporary boxcars but with sliding plug doors.

Piggyback trailers

As an increasing amount of produce traffic moved to trucks in the 1960s, some railroads and car owners attempted to regain business through piggyback service—which had been increasing rapidly since the late 1950s.

Among the largest owners were Fruit Growers Express and Pacific Fruit Express, **29**. Both acquired substantial fleets of 40-foot refrigerated trailers (3,300 for PFE by 1968). Other refrigerated-trailer operators included Southern Pacific, Missouri Pacific, and New York Central/MDT (Flexi-Van containers operated as trailers).

CHAPTER THREE

Car fleets and owners

A string of original (Armour-owned) Fruit Growers Express wood reefers pause at the Illinois Central's Water Street Yard in Chicago in 1917, two years before Armour was ordered to divest itself of its produce fleet. Also visible in the background are several Atlantic Coast Line ventilated boxcars. *Illinois Central*

By the turn of the 20th century, most refrigerator cars were controlled by private owners, mainly meatpacking companies. Railroads would soon get into ownership on a large scale, albeit indirectly via subsidiary companies.

2

PFE acquired 1,000 R-40-20 reefers in 1945. The 40-foot steel cars had 4/4 Dreadnaught ends and featured improved (fiberglass) insulation and floor racks. *Union Pacific*

In 1900, the largest refrigerator car owner was meatpacking giant Armour, with about 20,000 refrigerator cars—a majority of which were actually in produce service. Armour and other meat companies already had icing facilities in place around the country, and Armour, in particular, had figured out how to make money by leasing cars to produce shippers and then charging them for icing the cars in transit.

Many formal protests were filed by shippers and railroads against Armour, alleging unfair competition by Armour's requirement for railroads to use Armour equipment exclusively (and to route its meat cars over their routes to get preferential prices). This led to many railroads forming their own subsidiary companies to provide cars.

The situation was severe enough that in 1919 the Federal Trade Commission ruled against Armour. The FTC required that Armour divest itself of the portion of its refrigerator-car business not handling its own meat products, specifically its produce subsidiary, then named Fruit Growers Express, **1**.

The result was a sudden rush for railroads that had not already done so to form their own subsidiary companies to handle perishable traffic. Forming a subsidiary provided protection against the investment compared to owning cars outright. Private cars were also billed differently (by mileage) than railroad-owned cars, which used a per diem rate. Subsidiaries also allowed multiple railroads to share cars, getting better car utilization.

Refrigerator car ownership fell into three basic categories. First were railroads that chose to own at least a portion of cars directly. Northern Pacific, Illinois Central, and Bangor & Aroostook are examples.

Next were the separate operating/owning subsidiaries of individual railroads or groups of railroads. Pacific Fruit Express, Santa Fe Refrigerator Department, and Fruit Growers Express are examples. These subsidiaries provide cars to shippers on covered railroads and provide protective services (ice and heat, see chapter 5 for details).

The third type is leasing companies. These lease cars to railroads or individual shippers (mainly meat packers) but don't provide protective services. The biggest example is Union Refrigerator Transit.

The following are summaries of the largest produce car owners and operators—those that owned more than 2,000 cars at any given time. It's impossible to cover every car type or class owned by each (entire books have been devoted to some). Car numbers are provided for major classes of some, but this wasn't possible for many where cars were renumbered or where there were extensive series of cars. Some owners divided cars into classes (notably PFE and SFRD), while others did not, making them harder to organize.

Pacific Fruit Express

Pacific Fruit Express, established in 1906, became the nation's largest operator of refrigerator cars. The company was co-owned by Union Pacific and Southern Pacific, both controlled at the time by E. H. Harriman. In addition, Western Pacific signed a contract in 1923 for PFE to provide protective services.

Together UP and SP served a wide area that stretched from Washington and Oregon down through California and across Arizona and Texas. The multiple crops and harvest seasons in

Sliding plug doors began to replace swinging doors around 1950. PFE's 2,000 R-40-26 cars were built in 1951 and 1952.

J. David Ingles collection

these areas meant a shared car fleet would always remain active.

Upon startup, PFE purchased former Armour icing and repair facilities along both railroads. The company's first action was to order 6,600 new reefers from American Car & Foundry. Numbers 1–6600 were classes R-30-1 and R-30-2 (for PFE cars, R stood for refrigerator, 30 was ton capacity, and the last number was the design specification sequence for that car type and capacity). These 40-foot cars had wood sides, ends, framing, and roofs, with steel underframes having fishbelly side sills. Both were rebuilt with improved bunkers to become -2 cars.

Next came class R-30-5 in 1910–1911 (3,021 cars numbered 7001–10121) and R-30-6 (3,098 cars, 10122–13219). All were rebuilt in the late 1920s, including many of the early -2 cars, with new underframes and trucks.

More 30-ton wood cars followed, through the R-30-14 cars of 1926. The R-30-12, -13, and -14 cars totaled more than 20,000 and had taller side doors, Bettendorf steel underframes (no fishbelly center or side sills), steel framing, and outside metal roofs (photo 3 on page 7). These cars made

up the bulk of the PFE wood car fleet through the steam era. Many were eventually rebuilt (and given new classes) and ran into the 1960s.

Another 2,775 cars (PFE 50001–52775) owned by Western Pacific, built to -12 and -13 specs, were leased to PFE in 1923 as part of PFE's agreement to provide services on WP. These wore the PFE paint scheme but had WP heralds.

Next came 40-ton wood cars, the 2,000 cars of R-40-2 in 1928 (photo 1 on page 52). These shared the body design of earlier cars but with an upgraded underframe. The first 1,000 had new end-mounted power brake wheels, but the last 1,000 had the old vertical masts. These were rebuilt just before and after World War II. Steel body framing (still with wood body) began with class R-40-4 (500 cars in 1930).

From 1937 to 1947, PFE rebuilt 20,000 older wood cars. This could entail a new body with metal framing or replacement of wood components as needed, with updated fixtures. Features depended on the year rebuilt (fans, stage icing, collapsible bunkers, upgraded hatches with built-on plug, steel roofs, steel ends, and a power brake gear).

Steel cars arrived in 1936–1937 with 4,700 reefers of class R-40-10 (photo 8 on page 16). These had vertical sheet-and-post sides, square-corner 4/4 Dreadnaught ends, tabbed side sills, panel roofs, and wood running boards. Starting in 1950, these were upgraded with air-circulating fans, metal running boards, and stage icing.

In 1941, 1,000 similar cars (R-40-14) arrived. These had W-corner post (rounded-corner) 4/4 Dreadnaught ends, steel running boards, and new hatch covers with integral plugs. Another 1,000 similar cars (R-40-20) were delivered in 1944 and 1945, **2**.

PFE's largest class of reefers, the 5,000 cars of R-40-23, came from five builders in 1947 (photo 9 on page 16). They had improved 3/3 Dreadnaught ends, had air-circulating fans, were taller (13'-7") than earlier cars, and had improved insulation and sidewall flues. Another 3,000 similar cars (with diagonal-panel roofs), class R-40-25, were built in 1949.

The 2,000 R-40-26 cars of 1951–52 were PFE's first cars with sliding plug doors (Youngstown) and with fans mounted above the bunkers instead of at floor level, **3**. The last major group of ice cars were R-40-27 and -28 cars in 1957. These looked like -26 cars, but had a combination 4-foot sliding and 2-foot swinging door (-27, 1,700 cars) or 6-foot sliding and 2-foot swinging door (-28, 100 cars).

The newer ice cars survived into the 1970s. Some were converted to top-ice vegetable (TIV) service and ran after ice docks were shut down in 1973.

PFE's first mechanical reefers were 70-ton, 50-foot cars: the 25 cars of R-70-7 (300001–300025) in 1953. They had improved Dreadnaught 3/4 ends, 6-foot sliding plug doors, and smooth sides with straight side sills. They stood 14'-6" tall, about a foot taller than most ice cars. Roller-bearing trucks became standard with PFE mechanical cars.

The 500 cars of R-70-8 (300026–300125), R-70-9 (300138–300337), and R-70-10 (300513–300712) in 1953–1956 were similar to the -7s, but the car end with the refrigeration equipment was an early (square-corner) Dreadnaught end, while the opposite end was an improved Dreadnaught. Also, the louvered areas were different, taking up less space on the sides. The -10s were taller at 15'-0".

Two experimental 40-foot cars in 1958 (R-40-29 nos. 100001 and 100002) led to 500 R-40-30 cars in 1958 (100003–100502). Designed for either fresh produce or frozen lading, these were geared to smaller shippers. Another 1958 delivery was a group of 500 50-ton cars, class R-50-6 (nos. 300713–301212). Initially delivered as produce-only cars, they resembled R-70-8s.

The 52-foot R-70-11 (400001–400025) and R-70-12 (301213–302212) cars of 1961 featured welded construction with external side posts, with a post on either side of each door at an angle. Door width increased to 8 feet. They had internal load dividers and the -11s had cushion underframes.

Through the next decade, PFE acquired more than 10,000 modern reefers, 57-foot mechanical cars starting with the 1,000 cars of R-70-13 in 1963, **4**. These and all subsequent PFE cars were built by Pacific Car & Foundry, which would build similar cars for other owners through 1971.

Mechanical refrigerators grew larger in the 1960s, as shown by PFE no. 450611. The 57-foot, exterior-post car was built in 1963. *J. David Ingles collection*

Following the PFE split, Southern Pacific's cars were labeled SPFE. Number 457111 is one of 1,200 class R-70-20 cars built in 1969. *Robert Smaus*

Number 24594, built in 1928, is a class Rᴿ-7 car. It has wood sheathing, a 5-foot-wide door opening, and a conventional underframe. *Mainline Photos*

7

SFRD no. 5061 is a steel-sheathed 50-foot car with heavy insulation designed for frozen foods. Precool motors are attached at both ends. *Trains magazine collection*

8

The original fishbelly underframe is readily visible on class RR-28 no. 3502, rebuilt in 1940. The former wood car received steel sides and recessed Dreadnaught ends. *Mainline Photos*

9

Class RR-60 car no. 2213 was built in 1958. It has smooth (sheet-and-post) sides and a 6-foot-wide sliding plug door. *Santa Fe*

These cars all shared a similar appearance, with external side posts and Dreadnaught ends. The -13s had 8-foot doors and were the last cars with diagonal-panel roofs. From the -14s to the -19s, cars had peaked roofs (with small ribs between the panel seams) and 9-foot doors.

The roof changed to a rounded design with the 1,200 cars of the -20s in 1970, at first with alternating ribbed and plain panels and then switching to all ribbed. Also with the -20s, the door width increased to 10'-6".

The largest classes were the R-70-15 cars of 1965 (1,500, nos. 452001–453500) and -16s of 1966 (2,000, 453501–455500). The final PFE reefers came in 1971: 600 cars each of R-70-24 and -25 (nos. 459501–460700) (photo 19 on page 20).

In 1961, PFE began buying 40-foot refrigerated trailers, acquiring more than 3,300 through 1968 (photo 27 on page 25). They were notable as the first 13'-6"-tall piggyback trailers, a foot taller than standard. They were built by Brown, Fruehauf, Strick, Timpte, and Trailmobile in a variety of styles. Just over 2,100 of these were actually containers on removable bogies (similar to the New York Central Flexi-Van system). These had nose-mounted refrigeration units.

In addition to trailers, PFE also operated (owned or leased) more than 1,300 piggyback flatcars—the only refrigerator car line to do so. The flats were considered part of a pool on SP and UP, and they reverted back to those railroads by 1974.

With the decline of perishable traffic through the 1970s, PFE was split up in 1978. (In 1971, reporting marks had become SPFE or UPFE based on ownership, as the newer mechanical cars were all purchased by the railroads and leased to PFE.)

Cars were divided between the owners: UP became Union Pacific Fruit Express (see the Union Pacific entry), and PFE was kept as a wholly owned subsidiary of SP (cars lettered SOUTHERN PACIFIC FRUIT EXPRESS), 5. SP's business kept dwindling, and in 1985, PFE was officially dissolved with remaining cars transferred to SP

Number 51164, built in 1966, is from Santa Fe's largest class of mechanical cars, the 700 57-footers of Rr-89. It wears the late all-orange scheme. *J. David Ingles collection*

proper. SP, in turn, was absorbed by UP in 1996.

PFE reefers wore a yellow-orange color until 1929 and were orange after that, with red ends and roofs. The UP and SP heralds first appeared in 1922 (each on an opposite side of the car), and in 1926, the heralds of both railroads appeared on both sides. The specific heralds (and placement) changed over the years. In 1960, the heralds were moved to the left, with large stepped PACIFIC FRUIT EXPRESS lettering on the right.

Mechanical cars initially wore the same scheme, but with gray (and then aluminum) roofs. White became the standard roof color for mechanicals in 1964, and ends became orange in 1975. Starting with the R-70-20s, cars received the outlined (white letter) PFE on the right side.

Santa Fe Refrigerator Department

Santa Fe Refrigerator Despatch was incorporated as a subsidiary of the Santa Fe Railway in 1903, and it was

reorganized as Santa Fe Refrigerator Department in 1918. It was second only to Pacific Fruit Express in terms of car ownership.

The company started with about 4,000 older wood cars inherited from Santa Fe, and began acquiring 40-foot wood truss-rod underframe, archbar-trucked cars almost immediately. By 1918, SFRD operated about 9,000 cars.

SFRD settled on 40-foot wood cars with steel underframes by the 1920s. From 1920 to 1926, SFRD bought 10,500 cars following USRA designs, with wood sides, ends, and roofs, steel underframes, and fishbelly center sills. These cars were classes Rr-W, -X, -Y, -2, -3, and -4. These and later SFRD cars had 5-foot-wide door openings, compared to 4 feet for most other owners' cars.

Hatch covers on Santa Fe cars were hinged on opposite ends compared to other cars. Hinges were on the outboard ends so they opened toward the car, with platforms inboard of the hatch covers. The covers remained upright (just past vertical) when open,

also different than other cars (where the cover opened to lay flat on the roof).

Starting in 1927, SFRD ordered cars following American Railway Association (ARA) guidelines. These still had wood sides, ends, and roof, but with steel underframes as specified for ARA-design boxcars, with no fishbelly center sill. From 1927 to 1931, Santa Fe added 2,800 of these cars in classes Rr-5, -7, -9, and -11, **6**.

In 1931, SFRD acquired 100 50-foot cars (Rr-10). The frozen food market was developing in California in the mid-1930s, and in 1936, Santa Fe modified 10 of the 50-footers with heavy insulation for frozen food service. Following this, SFRD bought new steel, heavy-insulation cars from General American in 1937 (200 cars, class Rr-22) and 1940 (100 of Rr-30 and 50 of Rr-31 with longer bunkers), **7**. The Santa Fe then modified another 75 Rr-10 cars.

For the most part, Santa Fe rebuilt older cars with steel bodies instead of buying new steel cars. The first batch,

33

400 USRA-style cars, was completed in 1936–1937 as class Rr-19. They had inverse-corrugation Dreadnaught ends, Murphy steel panel roofs, and wood running boards with wood hatch platforms.

The SFRD did indeed buy some new 40-foot steel cars, starting with 500 class Rr-21 reefers in 1937 but acquired only another 1,100 new steel cars through 1953.

Rebuilding of the USRA cars continued, with more than 10,200 cars completed through 1950. These can be spotted by their fishbelly underframes. The SFRD then rebuilt 2,800 ARA-style cars from 1950–1954. These, class Rr-49 to -55, were about 8" taller than the USRA rebuilds (photo 15 on page 19). They lacked fishbelly center sills and received sliding plug doors instead of the swinging doors of the earlier rebuilds.

The rebuilt USRA classes had varying features. Classes Rr-19 to -27 had full hatch platforms; abbreviated versions were used thereafter (the platform was eliminated between the hatch and car end). Metal running boards debuted with Rr-35.

The Dreadnaught car ends were recessed 4/4 style through Rr-32, standard 4/4 from Rr-33 to -40, and improved 3/3 from Rr-43 on, **8**. Murphy panel roofs were used through Rr-43, with diagonal panels thereafter. The side top sill was 3" wide through Rr-34, and 7" wide from Rr-35 to -48.

Santa Fe's first mechanical reefers were 30 cars, class Rr-54, in 1953. The SFRD called them MTC (mechanical temperature control) cars. Class Rr-56 cars arrived in 1955–56, followed by similar Rr-60 and Rr-61 cars through 1960, **9**. These 200 54-foot cars had smooth sides and 6-foot Camel sliding doors. The 100 cars of Rr-65 (SFRC 1100–1199), built by the railroad's Wichita Shops in 1960, had a wider door (8-foot Superior) and pronounced raised strips over the side vertical rivets (photo 7 on page 10).

The most common early MTC cars were the combined 600 cars of Rr-66 (SFRC 1000–1099, built 1960) and Rr-69 (1200–1699, built 1961), which shared a common appearance. Built by General American, they were the first cars with exterior-post sides.

The Rr-71 and Rr-72 (the latter with Super Shock Control underframes) cars of 1962 were built at Topeka. They were 2 feet longer than the previous cars and had angled side posts on either side of each door.

The next major groups were the Rr-77 (2300–2499) and Rr-83 (2500–2799) cars of 1963, both 57 feet with 9-foot doors, followed by 300 Rr-86 and 395 Rr-87 cars in 1964 and 1965. Santa Fe's largest class of mechanical cars was Rr-89 (50700–51399), 700 cars built in 1966, **10**. They also

11 Fruit Growers Express built many of its own cars starting in the 1920s. The company bought underframes and then built 40-foot wood bodies atop them. *Trains magazine collection*

12 FGE, Burlington Refrigerator Express, and Western Fruit Express all shared this design for plywood-sheathed cars during World War II. The long grab irons are a spotting feature. *Trains magazine collection*

13 In 1949, Pacific Car & Foundry rebuilt 100 older FGE 40-foot wood cars with steel bodies, plug doors, and fans. *Pacific Car & Foundry*

14

The last FGE mechanical cars were 65-foot smooth-side cars. Number 12751 was built in 1972. It wears the final white SOLID COLD scheme. *Jeff Wilson collection*

57-footers and the first delivered without running boards.

The last MTC cars were the 61-foot cars of Rʀ-90 (55200–55399, 1968), Rʀ-91 (55400–55699, 1969), Rʀ-92 (57000–57098, 1969), Rʀ-94 (55700–55899, 1970–71), Rʀ-95 (55900–56299, 1971), and Rʀ-96 (56300–56699, 1972), each with 10' or 10'-6" doors. They were built at Topeka, except for the Rʀ-91 and -92 cars, which were built by PC&F.

The SFRD bought nonrefrigerated, insulated (RBL) cars in 1955, 300 50-foot cars from Pullman-Standard (SFRB 6000–6299). The railroad acquired another 2,000 insulated cars by the early 1960s, mainly homebuilt (Topeka shops) cars and cars rebuilt from older boxcars. Most were 50-footers, except for 62 rebuilt 40-foot cars. Insulated cars had reporting marks SFRB, SFRA, and SFRE. Most were reclassified from bunkerless refrigerators to insulated boxcars (XLI, XMI) in the mid-1960s and renumbered with ATSF reporting marks.

Fleet size dropped from the 1960s onward. In 1980, the Santa Fe renamed the refrigerator car division the Perishable Traffic Development Department. The railroad retired its last mechanical reefers in 1988, using

FGE cars to cover the little traffic that remained. A small revival came in 1995 just before the BNSF merger when the railroad (through Santa Fe Leasing Corporation) leased 400 FGE mechanical cars and gave them SFLC reporting marks.

Santa Fe ice cars were orange with black ends, roofs, and trucks. The sides carried a variety of lettering variations, heralds, maps, and slogans. Early cars had a small square ATSF logo, with various train name slogans on one side and a map on the other (left) side.

Mechanical cars were orange with a large circle herald on the left and a dark blue door with an MTC graphic. These became all orange by the mid-1970s.

Insulated (RB, RBL) cars were initially mineral red with yellow doors; cars with Shock Control underframes were painted Indian Red (as were boxcars) but with orange doors.

Fruit Growers Express

Fruit Growers Express (FGE) was formed in 1920 following the breakup of the Armour refrigerator car line. It was a new company, even though it kept the old Armour subsidiary name, and adopted FGEX reporting marks. FGE started with about 4,200 former Armour wood cars.

Initially, FGE had 10 owners, but the company eventually provided services for more than 20 railroads. Major owners included Atlantic Coast Line, Baltimore & Ohio, Chesapeake & Ohio, Florida East Coast, Louisville & Nashville, New Haven, Norfolk & Western, Pennsylvania, Seaboard Air Line, and Southern. The company provided cars and protective services for the majority of perishable loadings east of the Mississippi River, particularly Florida and the Southeast. Its shops were in Alexandria, Va., and Jacksonville, Fla.

In addition, FGE operated as a consortium with Burlington Refrigerator Express (BRE, formed in 1923) and Western Fruit Express (WFE, formed in 1926). The three operated as a single company, pooling cars based on traffic. The three sometimes used common car designs and coordinated numbering for refrigerator cars. Each had its own repair facilities, but they shared directors, billing, and administrative functions.

Thoroughly tracking all of FGE's cars would require a book unto itself. Its early wood cars represented a wide variety of sizes and styles, as they came from more than a dozen railroads as they joined FGE. Most early wood

FGE acquired a substantial fleet of insulated boxcars. Number 81166 is a 45-foot car built by AC&F in 1955 and leased to Chesapeake & Ohio. *J. David Ingles collection*

cars, including all-wood designs (many truss-rod cars) acquired at startup, were retired by the late 1930s.

Significant groups of wood cars from other railroads included 2,600 36-foot RF cars from the Pennsy (in 1926) and 1,612 from B&O (1925). A distinctive early group were the 3,244 Pennsy R7 cars in 1932 (photo 6 on page 15).

FGE built many of its own cars, buying underframes from several sources and then building superstructures atop the frames in its own shops. The company built 100 new wood reefers in 1921–22 (nos. 32000–32099), followed by many more, **11**. Most of its new reefers were 40-foot cars with wood-sheathed ends and sides, wood roofs, and straight underframes with a 6"-wide (early) or 8"-wide (late) side sill. Early cars were 12'-1" tall, and later cars were 12'-10".

The company's first 150 steel reefers came in 1938 (10850–10999), rebuilt from old USRA boxcars. These 40-foot cars had vertical side sheathing, Murphy 5/5/5 ends, fishbelly underframes, and Hutchins roofs. Wartime restrictions on steel led FGE to build 374 plywood-sheathed cars from 1942 to 1946 (38000–38373). These had Dreadnaught ends and Murphy roofs, **12**.

More 40-foot steel cars arrived in 1946: 125 cars based on the earlier

plywood cars but with riveted steel sheathing (38375–38499), straight side sills, and 4/4 Dreadnaught ends. Next came 135 cars with horizontal side panels and improved Dreadnaught ends (38500–38634) in 1947–1948.

Two groups (665 total) of welded-side 40-footers came in 1949. Numbers 38635–38999 had tabbed side sills and Murphy panel roofs, and 39000–39299 had straight sills and diagonal-panel roofs. Another group of 700 cars began appearing in 1949 (39300–39999), and these had riveted vertical side panels, straight sills, and improved Dreadnaught ends.

New sliding plug-door cars came in 1951: 960 40-foot cars with 6-foot-wide doors from Pacific Car & Foundry (FHIX 40001–40960). Another 280 arrived in 1954 (FHIX 40961–41240), identical to the earlier cars but with taller (by 5") doors. PC&F had earlier (1949) rebuilt 100 wood cars with plug doors (FGEX 59900–59999), **13**.

Fruit Growers Express bought its first 25 mechanical cars in 1949 to tap the growing frozen orange juice traffic in Florida. FGE soon had about 150 mechanical cars, and most were 52 feet long: 151–199, 209–249, and 340–399, plus a few experimental cars. FGE also had a batch of 50 42-foot mechanical cars (250–299).

In 1954, FGE bought the first 100 of what would eventually become 600 (1000-series) 52-foot all-purpose cars (photo 16 on page 19). These smooth-side cars had 3/4 Dreadnaught ends, straight side sills, 6-foot plug doors, and roller-bearing trucks.

The 1960s saw 100 55-foot cars with 8-foot doors (10100–10199) and 200 64-foot cars with 9-foot doors (11000–11199). Another 500 similar cars (but 6" taller) came in 1968 (11200–11699). All had smooth sides.

In 1969, FGE began building 65-foot mechanical cars with smooth sides, Dreadnaught ends, and 10'-6" plug doors (similar cars went to WFE/BN and Frisco) and built them through 1972 (nos. 11700–12924), **14**. Cars had slight variations: welded or riveted sides and straight or angled side sills. These had FGCX reporting marks but were relettered FGMR starting around 1980.

The first of what would eventually become FGE's substantial fleet of bunkerless (RBL) cars were 45-footers from 1952 to 1955 (RBNX 80000–81499). They were taller than ice cars and had 8-foot sliding plug doors, **15**.

More 45-footers followed, staying in the 80000 series, with 55-footers following in the 90000 series, **16**. All the insulated cars had RBNX reporting marks. The RBLs were often leased to specific railroads and sometimes received the railroad's reporting marks.

By the early 1980s, FGE had about 1,200 mechanical cars and 600 insulated cars. The roster declined over the next decade, and in the early 1990s, the mechanical cars were all disbursed, going to BNFE (350), Santa Fe (400), UP (250), and Wisconsin Central (100).

Like PFE, FGE bought refrigerated piggyback trailers starting in 1960, **17**. They were aluminum with simple FRUIT GROWERS EXPRESS lettering. All were 40-footers, and early cars had curbside (right-hand) side doors. More than 2,400 were in service by 1967, but most were gone by the early 1970s.

The basic FGE color scheme was yellow sides, freight car red ends and roof, and black trucks, with FRUIT GROWERS EXPRESS spelled out on the left and the type of car spelled out on the right. After about 1950, some roofs were metallic silver or yellow.

Lettering on the mechanicals in 1969 swapped sides for the spelled out name and added FOR GREATEST EFFICIENCY lettering. Around 1980, the scheme changed to white with shadow FGE initials on the left and SOLID GOLD on the right.

Insulated cars were initially similar, but with two horizontal stripes bracketing the FRUIT GROWERS EXPRESS and INSULATED lettering. Later RBL cars shared the shadow FGE initials but on a yellow car with SOLID GOLD lettering.

Western Fruit Express

Western Fruit Express (reporting mark WFEX) was formed by the Great Northern in 1923, with shops in Hillyard, Wash., and St. Paul, Minn. The company (along with Burlington Refrigerator Express) operated as an affiliate of Fruit Growers Express and shared offices in Washington, D.C.

Upon startup, WFE inherited GN's reefer fleet, the core of which were about 4,000 40-foot, 25-ton cars built in the 1910s and 1,000 similar 30-ton cars built in 1921–22 by General American (nos. 49000–49999). These had truss-rod underframes—surprising for the 1920s order, **18**.

Around 1980, FGE began applying the SOLID GOLD scheme to insulated cars. This one, leased to Seaboard Coast Line (with SCL reporting marks), is shown in 1982. *Kenneth R. Combs*

Fruit Growers Express bought refrigerated trailers from 1960 through 1967. This 40-foot trailer was built by Dorsey in 1967. *Dorsey*

Western Fruit Express had 1,000 40-foot wood cars, with steel center sills and truss rods, built in the early 1920s. Some ran through the 1950s. *Trains magazine collection*

Many older WFE wood cars were rebuilt in the late 1940s. Number 72316 received steel sides with straight sills, a diagonal-panel roof, and improved 3/3 Dreadnaught ends. *J. David Ingles collection*

The earlier cars were modified with steel center sills in 1924–1925 but retained their truss rods, giving them a distinctive appearance. Some of the rebuilt cars (renumbered 60001–63910) lasted through the 1950s, and some also received steel roofs before retirement. The General American cars received steel underframes in the early 1930s, and some were further rebuilt in the 1940s and renumbered in the 71000 and 73000 series.

Just over 2,000 new 40-foot wood cars with steel underframes were built in 1924 and 1926 (65000–66349) and from 1928 to 1932 (67000–67894). Many were rebuilt, many with steel bodies, in 1948–1949 and renumbered in the 71000 to 73000 series, **19**.

WFE built its first 50 all-steel cars in 1936 (67895–67944). World War II saw 225 plywood-sheathed cars built from 1942 to 1946 (same design as the FGE car in photo **12**). Many were rebuilt in the 1950s with conventional tongue-and-groove siding.

Additional 40-foot steel cars included 175 from Mt. Vernon (66625–66799) in 1946 and 1,500 from Pacific Car & Foundry in 1948–1951 (68000–69492). Cars built starting in 1950 (beginning with 68650) had sliding plug doors.

The last WFE ice-bunker cars were 840 40-foot, 70-ton cars (70000–70839) for frozen food service, **20**. Built by PC&F from 1952–1955, they had extra-heavy insulation and 6-foot sliding plug doors. They received WHIX reporting marks, with HI standing for Heavy Insulation.

WFE added just over 600 insulated cars to its fleet from 1955 through 1964, all with RBWX reporting marks (63000–64561). Most were 50-foot, 60-ton cars with 8-, 9-, and 10-foot sliding plug doors, but nos. 63000–63099 were 60-foot, 80-ton cars.

In 1962–1963, 200 older 49000-series wood cars were rebuilt for bulk potato loading. These (WFBX 71784–71974) had interior slope sheets, conveyor chains, and heaters. They were followed by another 510 converted from steel cars (WFBX 71274–71783) from 1965–1968.

The first WFE mechanical cars were built by FGE: 40-footers 890–899 in 1952 and 50-footers (70-ton) 800–849 in 1953. Another 150 50-foot cars (7950–8099) arrived from 1954–1957 and then 50 40-foot cars (7900–7949) in 1957, **21**. All had 6-foot sliding plug doors, and all built in 1953 and later had roller-bearing trucks. Another 100 50-foot cars built by FGE in 1961 had 8-foot doors and internal load dividers (WFCX 8100–8199).

All subsequent GN-controlled WFE cars were built by PC&F. All were 57-foot, 70-ton cars, including 100 in 1963 (WFCX 8200–8299) similar to PFE R-70-13 with 8-foot doors; 600 from 1964–1967 with 9-foot doors (8300–8999) similar to PFE R-70-14, and 200 in 1969 (9000–9199) following PFE R-70-20, with 10'-6" doors, **22**.

In 1970, Great Northern became part of Burlington Northern. All Northern Pacific and Burlington Refrigerator Express reefers became part of the WFE fleet.

Under BN ownership, another 500 57-foot cars arrived, including WFCX 9200–9249 and 9300–9699 from PC&F, and WFCX 9250–9299 from FGE's shops, **23**. The FGE cars had smooth sides, while PC&F cars had external posts.

Ice-bunker cars were retired soon after the merger, and in 1973, all WFE cars began receiving BNFE reporting marks. All subsequent cars were owned by BN, although some kept WFE sublettering.

The WFE paint scheme was yellow sides, mineral red ends and roof, and black underframes and trucks. Sides featured WESTERN FRUIT EXPRESS lettering and a round GN herald. This evolved to gothic lettering and a revised herald in 1967 and the eventual change to BN green. By the late 1980s, BN cars were painted white.

Burlington Refrigerator Express

Burlington Refrigerator Express (reporting mark BREX) was formed in 1926 to take over refrigerator car operations on the Chicago, Burlington & Quincy, with primary shops at Plattsmouth, Neb. It was affiliated with—and operated cars in a pool with—Western Fruit Express and Fruit Growers Express.

Upon startup, BRE inherited about 3,000 cars from the Burlington, renumbering them to the 70000 series. Some were older 32- to 36-foot cars, but the majority were 40-foot wood cars with a mix of steel underframes, steel center sills, and all-wood truss-rod cars.

The largest group of original cars included 1,300 40-foot cars built in 1922–1923. The fishbelly underframe cars followed American Car & Foundry's basic design of the period but came from three builders (AC&F, Pullman, and General American), **24**. Most truss-rod cars were retired or moved to company ice service by the end of the 1940s.

In 1932, Burlington subsidiaries Colorado & Southern and Fort Worth & Denver joined BRE. Cars of these lines received CX and FWDX reporting marks.

BRE's first new cars arrived in 1937—270 steel 40-foot cars (nos. 74730–74999), built at Plattsmouth, **25**. They had 10-panel steel sides with tabbed side sills, square-corner Dreadnaught ends (with forked-end ribs), and panel roofs.

World War II restrictions led to BRE building 298 cars with conventional tongue-and-groove wood siding in 1942–1945 (74400–74697). These had Dreadnaught 3/4 ends, Murphy panel roofs, and fans. Some later received plywood sheathing.

More steel cars came in 1949–1950 (74200–74399). These 40-foot, 50-ton cars had straight side sills, improved Dreadnaught 3/3 ends, and distinctive door latches that angled downward

20

Pacific Car & Foundry built 840 cars with heavy insulation and sliding plug doors in the early 1950s for frozen food service. They had WHIX marks (with HI for Heavy Insulation). *Jeff Wilson collection*

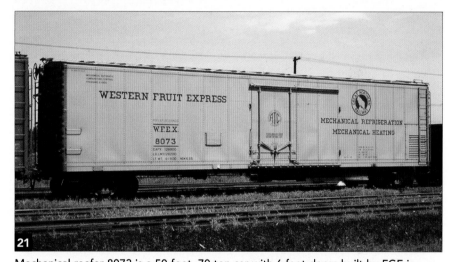

21

Mechanical reefer 8073 is a 50-foot, 70-ton car with 6-foot doors built by FGE in 1955. It shares a body style with contemporary FGE and BRE cars. *J. David Ingles collection*

22

Number 8465 is a 57-foot, exterior-post mechanical car with 9-foot doors built by PC&F in the mid-1960s. It's similar to PFE's R-70-14 design. *J. David Ingles collection*

23 Although it carries BNFE reporting marks, no. 19622 still carries WFE lettering on the right. The car was built by PC&F in 1971. *Jeff Wilson collection*

when secured. BRE's last ice cars arrived in 1951–1952: 350 sliding-plug-door 40-footers (76000–76349) built by Indiana Harbor and PC&F, **26**.

The first 30 BRE mechanical cars, in 1953, were built by FGE (BREX 120–149). These smooth-sided 55-foot cars had roller-bearing trucks and sliding plug doors. Another 70 were built at Burlington's Havelock Shops in 1957 (5000–5069) following an FGE design also used by WFE, **21**.

In 1963, BRE acquired 100 56-foot mechanical cars with outside bracing and 8-foot doors. These were divided between meat service (BRMX 5100–5149) and general service (BRCX 5150–5199). The last BRE mechanicals came in 1966: 200 67-foot cars (BRMX 5200–5299 and BRCX 5300–5399). These cars had 10-foot doors and hydraulic-cushion underframes.

BRE built its first insulated nonrefrigerated (RBL) cars in 1957, 100 50-foot cars built at Havelock (RBBX 79000–79099). The 70-ton cars had smooth sides with straight sills, 8-foot sliding plug doors, interior load dividers, and cushion underframes. Many additional RBL cars followed through the 1960s,

including 300 60-foot, external-post cars (RBBQ 78000–78299) with 10-foot doors.

With the Burlington Northern merger in 1970, BRE cars became part of the Western Fruit Express fleet.

The standard BRE paint scheme was yellow sides with mineral red ends and roofs (silver roofs after 1949) and black underframe and trucks. Sides carried BURLINGTON REFRIGERATOR EXPRESS lettering on the left with the Burlington herald on the right. EVERYWHERE WEST and WAY OF THE ZEPHYRS lettering (on opposite sides) began appearing in 1949. Insulated cars were green with a yellow horizontal band.

Merchants Despatch Transportation

Merchants Despatch Transportation (MDT) had its beginnings in the 1800s as a freight forwarder over New York Central lines. Its history and corporate structure are complex. Starting in 1896, it was building cars of many types at East Rochester, N.Y.

MDT provided a mix of cars under lease and/or protective services for NYC lines and more than 20 other railroads for varying periods of time,

including Bangor & Aroostook; Delaware, Lackawanna & Western; Gulf, Mobile & Ohio; Illinois Central; Kansas City Southern; Missouri-Kansas-Texas; Northern Pacific; and St. Louis-San Francisco. Included were arrangements with other car owners (including Pacific Fruit Express) to provide cars in reciprocal arrangement for peak demands.

In addition, MDT leased cars to a variety of private owners, including breweries, dairies, meat packers, food distributors, and manufacturers (often with reporting marks for the lessee). Many of these into the early 1930s were billboard-style cars.

In 1923, MDT operated just over 10,000 wood cars, **27**. About 3,200 were 36-footers and the remainder were 40-foot cars. The 30-ton 36-footers, built from the 1890s through 1909, were rebuilt in the 1920s with steel center sills and upgraded doors. Some lasted into the 1940s, many of these in meat service. The modern 40-footers had wood sides, ends, and framing; Murphy outside-metal roofs; and steel fishbelly center sills.

More than 9,000 wood 40-foot cars were built through 1930, including

MC 16250–16999 (Michigan Central), NYC S146000–S146999, NKP 60000–60399 (Nickel Plate), B&M 13100–13299 (Boston & Maine), and MDT 17000–22749, 3000–3499, and 4000–4999. Many were renumbered in 1940s (to 40000–47999) when upgraded with AB brakes.

In 1928, MDT acquired Northern Refrigerator Car Co. but kept operating it separately (as Northern Refrigerator Line). In 1936, Despatch Shops was spun off and became the main construction and repair shops for all types of cars on NYC and affiliates.

Two new batches of wood cars in 1930 (MDT 3500–3699) and 1931 (MDT 5000–5999) appeared similar but with conventional steel underframes, **28**. The last 50 cars of the 1931 order had Dreadnaught ends, as did all following cars. Another 1,600 similar cars arrived through 1941 (non-meat cars included MDT 6000–6499, 7000–7499, and 8000–8149).

MDT rebuilt many cars in the mid-1950s with fans. Some wood cars also received steel sides (10-panel with straight side sills), some with sliding plug doors. All cars were subject to renumbering and new reporting marks. (MDT also operated cars with ERDX reporting marks, for Eastern Refrigerator Despatch.)

The first MDT-lettered steel reefers came in 1947, 475 40-foot cars (9000–9474), **29**. They had tabbed sills, panel roofs, Dreadnaught 3/4 ends, and fans. More 40-footers arrived in 1948 (MDT 9475–9974), 1948-1954 (MDT 10000–12699), and the last ice cars, built by PC&F in 1956 and 1958 (MDT 13000–13749 and 14000–14049), **30**.

Variations included 40 of the 1948 cars receiving sliding plug doors, with proprietary Despatch ends on the 1951 and later Despatch-built cars (no. 11000 onward). The last 50 PC&F cars of 1958 had 4-foot sliding doors adjacent to a 2-foot swinging door over a 6-foot opening.

MDT owned very few mechanical cars: 50 smooth-side, 50-foot cars with sliding plug doors built by PC&F in 1956 (NYMX 1000–1049) plus a single car (NYMX 2000) rebuilt by

Colorado & Southern 99726, in company ice service by this late 1950s photo, shares the design of parent Burlington's early wood cars with a fishbelly underframe. *J. David Ingles collection*

BRE's first steel cars, built in 1937, had early square-corner Dreadnaught ends, tabbed side sills, and panel roofs. *Mainline Photos*

Burlington's last ice cars had sliding plug doors. The 40-foot, 50-ton cars had fans and 3/3 improved Dreadnaught ends and were built in 1951–1952. *Big Four Graphics, Jay Williams collection*

27

Merchants Despatch built several thousand 40-foot wood (steel underframe) cars in the 1910s. This one, rebuilt in 1920, was one of 1,000 built in 1913. *New York Central*

28

Number 5721, built in 1931, is a modern MDT wood car with a conventional steel underframe. Shown here in Chicago around 1940, it wears the 1939 yellow paint scheme. *John Vachon, Library of Congress*

29

MDT resurrected the white scheme for its 475 steel cars delivered in 1947, including no. 9061. *Trains magazine collection*

Despatch Shops from an older car in 1958.

Most of the steel ice-bunker cars lasted through the 1960s but were retired as ice service ended through the 1970s.

The original MDT scheme was white sides with red and blue stripes, boxcar red ends and roof, and black underframe and trucks. Sides became yellow on wood cars in 1939. The white scheme was revived in 1947 from the first steel cars through 1951, changing to orange after that. Cars had reporting marks, number, and (after 1947) the MDT logo on the left, with REFRIGERATOR and—on some cars—the NYC logo to the right of the door. This was simplified in 1956 with sans-serif lettering, and after that, the logo on the right could be the NYC or a leasing railroad.

The mechanical cars were yellow with a wide blue horizontal band and silver ends and roof, and some were later repainted yellow.

American Refrigerator Transit

American Refrigerator Transit (ART) was an early private-car owner, getting its start in 1881. It was co-owned by Missouri Pacific and Wabash (MoPac held 75 percent ownership in the 1940s), and also covered the Denver & Rio Grande Western. Its headquarters and major shops were in St. Louis. Its primary traffic source was produce from the Rio Grande Valley of Texas, but it also carried produce, meat, and dairy products originating throughout the Midwest and plains states.

Early cars included a variety of 32-, 36-, and 38-foot truss-rod reefers. The company was an early customer of American Car & Foundry, buying 1,000 steel-underframe (fishbelly) 40-foot cars in 1911 (nos. 11000–11999). Another 2,000-plus cars arrived in 1912–1913 (12000–14099) and 2,000 in 1922 (15000–16999).

The next cars, 755 built in 1924 (17000–17749 and 18950–18954), followed the common popular AC&F design of the time, and more than 3,700 more followed in 1927 to 1930 (19000, 20000, 21000, and 22000 series) (photo 4 on page 14). The 1922

cars with 8-foot doors coming in 1960 (300–399). During this time, the NP also bought a batch of 25 40-foot cars (501–525), delivered in 1958, **38**.

All remaining NP reefers came from PC&F, including NPM 400–449 in 1961, 52-foot cars distinctive for their partial external-post construction (three posts on either side of the 8-foot door). Next were nos. 450–499, delivered in 1962, with 8-foot doors, smooth sides, internal load dividers, and a 68-ton capacity.

Numbers 526–550, built in 1963, were 57-foot cars with external-post sides, 8-foot doors, and Hydra-Cushion underframes. They were followed by additional 57-footers with 9-foot doors: 551–975 and 1500–1599 from 1964–67. Northern Pacific's final reefers were 50 57-foot cars with 10'-6" doors, delivered in 1969.

The railroad also acquired several hundred bunkerless (RBL) insulated cars starting in 1957, including 40- and 50-foot cars with sliding plug doors. Many of these were designed for transporting potatoes and included suspended hooks for portable heaters, **39**.

With the NP's merger into Burlington Northern in 1970, NP reefers became part of the Western Fruit Express fleet.

The NP's ice cars were yellow with boxcar red ends, black underframes and trucks, arched road name, and Monad herald. Mechanical cars were silver with black underframes and trucks. Bunkerless RBLs were dark green with a thin yellow horizontal stripe. The first steel cars began carrying MAIN STREET OF THE NORTHWEST script lettering below the Monad, and starting with the 1954 steel cars SCENIC ROUTE OF THE VISTA DOME NORTH COAST LIMITED lettering.

Illinois Central

Illinois Central operated its own refrigerator cars and also leased cars as needed through Northern Refrigerator Line (and Merchants Despatch, after MDT acquired NRC).

The backbone of IC's fleet through the 1930s was a roster of about 5,000 40-foot, 30-ton wood cars built by

Built in 1958, NP's 40-foot mechanical refrigerator cars had 6-foot sliding doors. The silver scheme was standard on NP mechanical cars. *J. David Ingles collection*

Northern Pacific's insulated boxcars wore green with a yellow stripe. Number 98604, a 40-foot car with 8-foot door, was built at the railroad's Brainerd, Minn., shops in 1959. *J. David Ingles collection*

Illinois Central 53190, a 40-foot wood car with a steel underframe built by AC&F in 1916, was typical of the railroad's reefer fleet into the 1930s. *American Car & Foundry*

Number 50456 is from the second batch of IC steel reefers, built in 1942. Shown here in fresh paint in 1960, the car had air-circulating fans added in the early 1950s. *J. David Ingles collection*

American Car & Foundry in the teens, **40**. They were originally numbered in seven series from 53001 to 59999. By the 1940s, the IC was down to about 1,500 wood cars, and most wood cars were off the roster by the mid-1950s.

The IC bought its first 300 steel reefers (nos. 50000–50299) in 1937. Built by General American, the 40-ton cars had tabbed side sills, square-corner Dreadnaught ends, and panel roofs. They became known as "banana cars," as their main duty was carrying bananas north from New Orleans. Another 200 steel cars came from General American in 1941–42 (50300–50499), with rounded (W-corner-post) Dreadnaught ends, **41**. None originally had fans, but these were applied starting in 1950.

By the 1950s, the IC was leasing a substantial number of NRC and MDT cars, and the IC logo began appearing on these cars starting in 1956, **29**. Cars were from a variety of NRC and MDT number series.

The IC's own reefers were yellow with a narrow dark green horizontal stripe across the bottom, with black ends and roof. The IC logo was on the left and the road name on the right. The MDT and NRC cars followed those owners' schemes, with the IC herald on the right.

Bangor & Aroostook

The Bangor & Aroostook signed a contract in 1924 with MDT to provide protective services for its significant potato traffic out of Maine. The railroad also used a fleet of wood boxcars with permanent underbody heaters for this service.

In the early 1950s, the railroad bought about 300 second-hand reefers from MDT. These were rebuilt 35-ton wood cars numbered in the 6000 series. The railroad also bought 1,200 40-foot steel cars with sliding plug doors, numbered 7000–7856 and 8000–8349, **42**. In the early 1960s, another batch of 275 second-hand steel 40-footers arrived

(numbered in the 8400 series). These cars had conventional swinging doors.

Because most of its spuds moved in the late fall and winter, heating was more important than refrigeration. The railroad bought new insulated/heated boxcars (AAR code XIH) in 1953, nos. 2000–2449, **43**. These wore the railroad's distinctive red, white, and blue STATE OF MAINE PRODUCTS scheme (which had appeared on the wood potato boxcars around 1950). When not carrying potatoes, these cars carried paper.

Mechanical cars arrived in 1963, with 50 57-foot cars from Pacific Car & Foundry (visually identical to PFE R-70-13 cars), nos. 100–149. Another 306 mechanical cars arrived through 1970, all from PC&F: nos. 94–299 and 50 cars each in the 11000, 11100, and 11200 series. The mechanical cars mainly carried frozen potato products.

The ice cars were out of service by the mid-1970s, but some mechanical cars lasted into the early 1990s.

The standard reefer scheme was orange with the BAR herald on the right. Later cars had large BAR initials (early wood cars first wore a blue and white scheme). The insulated cars were later repainted in the reefer scheme. In the early 1970s, the mechanicals received a spelled-out road name on the left and new herald on the right.

Union Pacific

When Pacific Fruit Express split in 1978, Union Pacific had more than 5,000 mechanical cars. The railroad's service officially became Union Pacific Fruit Express (UPFE and UPRX reporting marks). Cars were painted UP Armour Yellow, with UNION PACIFIC FRUIT EXPRESS in stepped style to the right of the door, with the UP herald on the left, 44. This was later simplified with just the herald on the right and large UPFE reporting marks on the left.

Many older cars were retired through the 1980s. The UP acquired additional former American Refrigerator Transit mechanical cars in 1982 when it absorbed the Missouri Pacific and later with groups of former Santa Fe and Fruit Growers Express cars in the 1990s (along with remaining Southern Pacific cars upon the UP/SP merger in 1996).

The UP in the late 1990s began rebuilding many cars with new refrigeration equipment, GPS, and remote temperature recognition, starting with many former ART and FGE cars. These were painted white with ARMN reporting marks, 45.

The UP purchased new 72- and 64-foot cars from Trinity beginning in 1998 and currently operates them along with several classes of rebuilt cars (photo 21 on page 22). The 1,500 new 64-footers are in the 110000 series, and 600-plus 72-foot cars are in the 170000 series. UP's fleet of 5,000-plus cars is by far the largest in operation as of 2018.

Railway Express Agency

Railway Express Agency (reporting mark REX) began acquiring its own express refrigerator cars in the 1940s, buying and leasing older wood and

42 The Bangor & Aroostook bought 1,200 40-foot steel reefers in the early 1950s. These cars had 6-foot sliding plug doors. *Bangor & Aroostook*

43 A batch of 450 40-foot insulated boxcars with underslung heaters arrived on the BAR in 1953. They initially wore the railroad's red, white, and blue scheme. *J. David Ingles collection*

44 This R-70-19 car was built in 1968. In 1985, it wears the Union Pacific Fruit Express scheme with outlined white initial letters. *Jim Hediger*

Union Pacific began rebuilding older refrigerator cars in the 1990s, painting them white with ARMN reporting marks. *Jeff Wilson*

Refrigerator car fleets for perishables

	1930	1940	1954	1962	1971	1978	1990	2001	2007	2016
ART	12,500	13,000	9,100	8,400	5,100	—	—	—	—	—
BAR	—	—	—	1,300	2,100	1,000	100	—	—	—
BRE[1]	2,400	2,000	2,000	1,700	—	—	—	—	—	—
BNFE[1]	—	—	—	—	—	4,500	1,800	—	—	—
BNSF[1]	—	—	—	—	—	—	—	2,000	1,800	980
FGE	18,100	14,400	12,500	12,400	7,900	2,800	—	—	—	—
IC[2]	5,000	2,100	620	560	640	20	—	—	—	—
MDT	11,900	13,000	8,700	10,100	5,900	1,000	—	—	—	—
NRC[3]	3,000	4,600	3,500	—	—	—	—	—	—	—
NWX	2,800	3,500	2,700	2,400	1,300	—	—	—	—	—
NP[1]	4,800	2,500	1,100	2,100	—	—	—	—	—	—
PFE[4]	40,500	37,700	39,000	24,100	17,800	1,900	—	—	—	—
REA	—	400	1,700	2,500	1,500	—	—	—	—	—
SFRD	18,300	14,100	14,800	12,900	9,600	4,600	—	—	—	—
SPFE[4]	—	—	—	—	—	4,800	2,700	—	—	—
UPFE[4]	—	—	—	—	—	5,700	3,800	5,300	5,900	5,200
URT	4,600	7,500	4,100	4,500	2,800	210	—	—	—	—
WFE[1]	7,200	7,100	5,700	5,700	9,800	700	—	—	—	—

[1] Burlington Refrigerator Express and Northern Pacific cars became part of Western Fruit Express in 1970. WFE became part of BNFE in the early 1970s, and BNFE became BNSF with the 1996 merger.

[2] Includes only cars owned by IC, not those leased from NRC or MDT.

[3] Northern Refrigerator Line (NRC) was acquired by MDT in 1962.

[4] PFE was split between SP and UP in 1978, becoming SPFE and UPFE. Cars are currently owned by UP with ARMN reporting marks.

No RB or RBL cars are included in totals after 1971, only ice or mechanical cars.

steel cars, **46**. REA's first new cars came from AC&F in 1947–1948 (nos. 6100–6599). The 55-foot, welded-side, plug-door cars were originally aluminum and green, but later repainted solid green (photo 24 on page 24). Another 500 similar (but riveted) cars (6900–7399) came from General American in 1955.

Another group of steel express reefers were rebuilt from former World War II troop sleepers in the late 1940s. In 1950–51, REA leased 300 of these cars (6600–6899), which can be spotted by their plated-over window openings on each side and their 5-foot swinging doors, **47**. They originally had Allied Full-Cushion trucks, which were swapped for other trucks in the late 1950s when the Allied trucks were banned.

REA still had 1,500 express reefers into the 1970s, but by then, they were used almost exclusively for nonrefrigerated shipments. All were retired when REA ceased operations in 1975.

Cars wore dark green with white lettering, and a large diamond logo by the early 1950s. In the early 1960s, this changed to a lighter green with simplified logo and REA EXPRESS lettering.

Other refrigerator car owners

Meatpacking companies, including Armour, Cudahy, Morrell, Swift, and Wilson, owned large fleets of refrigerator cars and leased many more from a variety of sources. These did not haul produce—they were in captive service among packing plants, branch houses, and distributors.

North American Car (NADX) owned 2,400 reefers in the early 1940s, largely leasing to packing companies and other private shippers. It acquired Mather and Western Refrigerator Line, among others, and was itself absorbed by GE Railcar in 1984.

Canadian Pacific and Canadian National both owned significant fleets of reefers (3,400 and 4,100 cars respectively in 1962), **48**. By the 1950s, most of their cars were overhead-bunker design with underbody-mounted heaters. They were used more in meat service than for perishables.

General American was better known as a railcar manufacturer, but it has long operated a substantial fleet of leased cars of several types. The company owned around 20,000 reefers by the 1930s and also owned leasing company Union Refrigerator Transit. Most of its own cars were leased to private owners, including breweries, meat packers (Swift's 5,000 cars were part of the GA fleet), and dairies, and many lessees had their own reporting marks. General American also was a major builder of express reefers and operated about 1,000 of them itself at one time.

Another major operator today is Cryo-Trans (photo 20 on page 22). The company started with a fleet of cryogenic (frozen carbon dioxide) cars in the late 1990s, eventually converting them to mechanical cars and adding many new cars to its fleet. The company owned almost 1,400 mechanical cars as of 2017.

Wood-sheathed express reefer 1257 was built by General American in the late 1920s. The 50-foot car was acquired by REA in the 1940s. *Mainline Photos*

Converted troop sleepers can be spotted by the plated-over window openings along the side. REA had 300 of these cars. *J. David Ingles collection*

Most Canadian refrigerator cars, like CN 212145, had overhead ice bunkers (brine tanks), meat rails, and underbody heaters. *J. David Ingles collection*

1

CHAPTER FOUR

Packing houses, harvesting, and loading

Refrigerator cars of both Pacific Fruit Express and SFRD await loading at the staggered docks of Continental Produce Co. in Los Angeles in July 1932. PFE 71991, left, is an R-40-2 car, and SFRD 24056, second from left, is an +Rʀ-5 car built in 1927. *University of Southern California Libraries/California Historical Society*

Once fruits and vegetables are harvested, the clock starts ticking on their freshness. Produce needs to be processed or refrigerated and shipped on its way to final users as soon as possible. This is why packing houses, packing sheds, and processing factories are located close to growing areas, **1**.

Orange groves are visible across the road from the LaVerne Cooperative Citrus Association packing house, one of California's largest in 1920. The large building features several rooms and multiple loading tracks. The rooftop refrigeration condenser unit (back center) marks it as having a cooling or cold storage room. *University of Southern California Libraries/California Historical Society*

Let's take a look at the key growing regions and see how harvest seasons fall in various areas of the country. We'll then examine how produce is harvested and prepped at packing sheds, and how various fruits and vegetables are loaded onto refrigerator cars for their journeys to market.

Seasons and harvests

The first commercial citrus grove in California was planted in 1841— a two-acre orchard. The expansion of settlers, the coming of railroads, and the development of the refrigerator car led to great opportunities for large-scale commercial operations for fruit and vegetables in California, Texas, Florida, and many other areas.

It can be difficult to grasp the huge scale of commercial citrus and truck farms, even back in the heyday of ice-bunker car operations in the 1940s and 1950s. In California alone, central region (Salinas Valley) lettuce growers harvested 136,000 acres each year—enough for more than 25,000 refrigerator carloads. In nearby Kern County, more than 750 growers each harvested at least 1,500 acres of potatoes, amounting to more than 30,000 carloads. And that was just two small areas in California. Almost every state produced some type of perishable in large enough quantities to require rail service.

California was (and is) the country's largest producer of fruits and vegetables. Something was being harvested every month of the year: asparagus in March and April; potatoes in May and June; pears, melons, and fresh grapes from July to October; tomatoes in September and October; celery from August to January; navel oranges through the winter; lettuce from late fall through March; and Valencia oranges from spring into summer—just to name a few examples.

California isn't alone. Florida became the country's No. 1 citrus producer in the early 1930s, with oranges and grapefruit harvested in winter to early spring, and tomatoes, cabbage, melons, and other crops throughout the year.

Washington apples (and many from Oregon) were shipped in large quantities from October through December. Potatoes from Idaho, North Dakota, Minnesota, and Maine were carried from late fall into winter.

Arizona grows a wide variety of perishables, harvesting lettuce and carrots through the winter, asparagus from March to April, and cucumbers from April to September. Over in Texas, the Rio Grande Valley produces a wide variety of vegetables including onions, spinach, cabbage, and carrots, along with grapefruit, in seasons ranging from October to June.

Workers pack field boxes with carrots near Holtville, Calif., in February 1939. The truck will soon haul the boxes to a nearby packing house. *Dorothea Lange, Library of Congress*

Farmers unload cabbages directly from wagons into refrigerator cars along the Norfolk & Western in 1934. The cars are from Fruit Growers Express and Western Fruit Express. *Norfolk & Western, Library of Congress*

In the Southeast, peaches generate a lot of traffic in Georgia and South Carolina from May through August, along with sweet potatoes from Mississippi to the Carolinas, and melons from Florida, Mississippi, and Georgia.

Strawberries were an important rail traffic source, usually carried via express. They're picked in Louisiana in March and April, in North Carolina in May, and through June in California. Cherries were another frequent express shipment, originating in California as well as Michigan and Utah.

There are many other significant growing areas that generated rail traffic, but you get the idea—listing all of them would require a book unto itself.

From field to packing house

Harvesting, whether done manually or with machines, requires care to keep produce in marketable condition for the longest time. Depending upon the product, time of day may be important (leafy greens and strawberries are best picked in the morning if possible). Some crops should be fully grown and ripe at harvest (apples), while others are picked when still green and left to ripen in storage (as bananas were through the 1950s).

Some perishables have a very narrow window in which they must be harvested for the best quality, whereas others have more leeway. Some have a very short life after picking (about a week for strawberries), while others will last longer (potatoes can be stored for two months in the proper conditions).

Packing houses are located near the fields, orchards, and growing areas they serve, **2**. Regardless of the product, the goal is to get fruits and vegetables from the field to the loading area within an hour or two after being harvested, so they can be prepped and processed and stored or shipped at their optimal preservation temperature and humidity, **3**.

Through the Depression years, fieldwork and harvesting for many crops was very labor intensive and was reliant on migratory workers. By World War II, machinery and mechanization became more of a factor. Larger and more efficient tractors and related machinery were used for planting, cultivating, and harvesting. Individual farms and operations were increasing in size.

Farm areas near cities were being taken over for housing and industry, but irrigation became available in many rural areas, especially in parts of California, Arizona, and Texas, leading to more land being cultivated.

To move harvested produce in the early 1900s, many individual farmers would bring their goods by horse and wagon to small packing sheds or rural loading areas along railroads. By the 1930s, operations were becoming larger, with trucks bringing in larger loads and the packing houses growing as well.

Rural loading

The simplest method of loading cars was found in rural areas away from metro areas, where the size of operations and amount of produce being moved didn't rate dedicated packing houses or sheds. Empty reefers would simply be parked on an available spur, siding, or team track near the farms or fields being served and loaded directly by trucks and wagons, **4**.

Into the 1910s, the key was local access: loading areas had to be a reasonable distance for a horse and wagon journey from a farm. By the 1920s and '30s, farm trucks were widely used, and they could haul more and cover longer distances.

The railroad would deliver cars to the loading area. Once cars were loaded, speed was important to ensure that the cars could be picked up by a local freight or switch job as soon as possible. The local would then take the cars to the nearest icing platform, where cars would receive initial icing. Another alternative, if conventional platforms were too distant, would be to have cars iced before delivery and then have them re-iced at the loading area by a truck.

Depending upon the commodity being hauled, workers could add top ice or ice individual cases and baskets (particularly for spinach, lettuce, and other leafy vegetables). To do this, a car

5 Bundles of burlap potato sacks are off-loaded from a Santa Fe boxcar to a flatbed truck at a loading area near Monte Vista, Colo., in 1939. *Library of Congress*

6 A Tidewater Southern local has just picked up three loads and dropped off five empties at a small skeleton-frame packing shed at Turner, Calif., in June 1972. *R. T. Sharp*

Workers pack apricots at an open-air packing shed near Brentwood, Calif., in January 1938. Note the temporary roof and the bulbs wired to open wires above the tables. *Dorothea Lange, Library of Congress*

The Florida Citrus Exchange packing house in Fort Pierce was a sizable frame building sheathed in corrugated metal. Don't forget the substantial electrical service needed, as well as tanks for water and fuel. *Arthur Rothstein, Library of Congress*

Several packing houses were located in close proximity to each other along the Santa Fe in Placentia, Calif. Styles varied from the frame building at left to the concrete structure at center. *Tom Baxter*

of ice would be delivered along with the empty cars. Ice would be chopped on the spot and shoveled in place as needed (see photo 11 on page 78).

For rural loading, packing materials (crates, baskets, cartons, and bags) would have to be delivered to the site by truck or rail, **5**.

Packing houses and loading sheds

No two packing houses are alike. The smallest were rudimentary open-walled sheds with roofs, built simply to provide a centralized, protected, and direct-transfer location between vehicles and railcars. Many were not much more than a single covered room used for collecting incoming produce from the field and hand-packing goods into cases, cartons, or sacks, **6**. Open-air sheds, with a solid roof but open sides (or framework with temporary fabric roof) were often found in warm areas, especially southern California and Florida, **7**. Small sheds might have an outbound rail dock with room for one or two refrigerator cars.

The largest packing houses were permanent, well-built structures with multiple rooms for washing, processing, packing, material storage, and product storage. Many had cold-storage areas and perhaps vacuum precooling capabilities. The LaVerne facility loaded out about 1,800 cars each year, **2**. These buildings could stretch hundreds of feet in each direction and handle several railcars at once, often with multiple tracks.

Construction methods varied widely by region, amount of traffic, and the types of produce handled. Wood construction was typical, with clapboard or board-and-batten siding. Buildings could also be covered by corrugated-metal sheathing, **8**. Brick or concrete was used for many larger structures by the 1920s, and those in the Southwest could feature stucco construction as well.

Older buildings often feature a variety of construction styles and include numerous additions, new buildings, and revisions. Many have been modified heavily through the years.

Other features included scales for weighing trucks, storage areas for crates and other supplies (often outdoors in temperate areas), and water tanks (either separate or on building roofs).

Some structures featured extensive signs. Most included, at minimum, the name of the local company or cooperative, and any national brands (such as Sunkist).

Rail access varied greatly. Many packing sheds simply have a single track alongside a long loading platform, which can be from one to five or six cars in length. A variation is to have parallel tracks. This requires passing through cars on the near track using bridge plates to span doorways of parallel cars.

Other variations included sheds with covered tracks and sheds with multiple tracks in a staggered (ladder) pattern.

Packing houses were found throughout growing areas, and multiple sheds were often clustered in groups—sometimes directly next to each other or on back-to-back lots, **9**. They could be small, privately owned operations, owned by larger companies that contracted with local growers or were run as cooperatives among multiple growers or shippers.

Through the ice-car era, most packing operations were small businesses. Few were known outside of their regions, although many California citrus packing houses were members of Sunkist (the California Fruit Growers Association), a large cooperative.

Cases and crates

Packaging evolved through the years. Into the 1930s, the traditional packing method for most fruits and vegetables was putting them in wood crates or baskets, with some products (notably potatoes and onions) packed in large sacks, **10**.

Crates varied in size by products. Most had colorful end labels with creative names and artwork. These cases were assembled either onsite by a boxing department or at nearby box factories that typically supplied a number of local packing houses (these and other box materials could arrive via

10 Orange crates are stacked on end in two layers, with a final horizontal layer. The top of the load is kept below the openings to the bunker (note the full load of ice). *Library of Congress*

11 Wooden crates were sturdy but labor intensive to assemble and close. A worker clamps the cover on a case of wrapped Florida grapefruit before tacking it in place. *Arthur Rothstein, Library of Congress*

12 Wood strips tacked to the crates ensure that these lemon crates will stay in place with airflow gaps between them. *Library of Congress*

Preco staged these photos in the 1940s to show how much more could be loaded in a fan-equipped car (oranges, right) compared to a non-fan car (cantaloupes, left). *Pacific Railway Equipment Co.*

railcar or truck). The thin, rough-cut wood was considered disposable, used once for transport, and discarded by the end purchaser or end user.

Shipping crates differ from field crates or field boxes, which were used to transport various types of produce from fields to packing houses or loading docks. These boxes were generally larger and sturdier. They were made of heavier wood and were reused, as were other crates used internally by packing houses and processing plants.

Wood shipping crates were sturdy, protected produce effectively, stacked well, and could be assembled with gaps between slats to allow air to flow through as needed for various products. Their downside was that they took a lot of space to store and a lot of labor to assemble, **11**.

Fiberboard and coated cardboard boxes began appearing in the 1930s and began seeing wide use by the

1950s (although some wood survived through the 1970s and later). Much of the reason was economical. Fiberboard and cardboard cases were less expensive and less labor intensive than wood crates. Cardboard cases can be shipped flat from the manufacturer to the user and be easily assembled on site.

They are lighter and take less space, representing less dead weight than wood crates. This lowers shipping costs and makes it possible to increase the amount of product in a given space (refrigerator car, truck interior, or warehouse).

A downfall was strength: Cardboard and fiberboard aren't as strong and lose strength when they become wet—such as in a refrigerator car. Early boxes sometimes were crushed, especially at the bottom of a stack in a car.

Another challenge was that cardboard cases, unless modified with air holes (which reduce strength), are tightly sealed, which can make them

harder to cool inside the car. Precooling (by vacuum or cold storage) at the packer helped this.

Another change by the 1950s and '60s was packing items in bags directly for retail sale. This meant packing produce in smaller bags and then placing these bags in a larger carton. This process varied by product.

Unless produce had been precooled at the packer, crates would be stacked in ice-bunker cars with some space between them so air could flow freely among them. This often meant tacking thin strips of wood to each row of crates to ensure they stayed in place, **12**. Otherwise, one hard switching move or some hard slack action could result in shifting and broken crates.

Depending upon the size and style of crate, they may be stacked on end or flat on top of each other. They were generally stacked no higher than the openings of the end bunkers to ensure good airflow.

Products that had been precooled could be stacked more tightly, as the surrounding air would maintain the cases' temperature, Crates could also be packed more tightly in fan-equipped cars, as forced airflow was markedly improved over non-fan cars, **13**. Cardboard boxes were generally stacked tightly, as they couldn't have wood strips tacked to them. Sacks were loaded to make sure that the underlying products were not damaged by the weight of the sacks on top.

Getting sacks and crates into cars was, into the 1950s, usually done with a common hand truck, **14**. Another popular system, especially at larger packing houses, was to place portable conveyors from the storage area into the car through the door opening, **15**. These were usually nonpowered, consisting of a framework with a series of free-rolling cylinders. Many were decidedly low tech, with cartons and crates often used to support the conveyors.

Forklifts, lift trucks, and pallets didn't become commonly used until loading mechanical refrigerators in the 1960s. Doors on most ice cars were just 4 feet wide, and the floor racks weren't strong enough to support a forklift.

As more mechanical cars were used for produce, loads increased in size to match the larger cars. Along with the larger interiors, loads could be packed higher and more tightly. Many new mechanical cars were equipped with load restraint devices, which had become common in boxcars by the 1950s, **16**.

Precooling

When harvested, fruits and vegetables hold a lot of heat. For most fruits and vegetables, it's important to lower their temperature as soon as possible to slow the ripening process and prevent spoilage. Placing warm produce directly inside a refrigerator car and letting it cool in transit is inefficient, as it can take a full day or more for the product temperature to drop.

The answer is precooling the load prior to transit. Chapters 5 and 6 talk about precooling facilities, which were first placed in service in the 1910s

14

Five sacks of spuds—100 pounds each—are wheeled across a bridge plate into a Santa Fe class RR-51 reefer in the 1950s. *Santa Fe*

15

Wooden crates of lettuce from the San Joaquin Valley are loaded aboard PFE reefers using portable conveyors. *Southern Pacific*

16 Load restraint gates and devices became common on mechanical reefers and insulated boxcars, which enabled crates to be stacked tightly and securely. *Santa Fe*

17 Potatoes were often delivered to the packing house or processing plant in bulk by truck, as with this custom side-dump body. The spuds go directly into a wash. *Santa Fe*

(photo 22 on page 97). These facilities use ductwork to blow a large volume of cold air through a car and cool its load in an hour or two.

Another method, prior to the advent of air-circulating fans in cars, was placing portable electric fans inside the cars in front of the bunker openings to force cold air through the load. In the 1940s, as cars with built-in fans became common, precooling motors could be attached outside the car to power the car's fans (photo 13 on page 18).

Cold storage was another option—simply storing the produce in a cold room to lower its temperature prior to loading. This worked well, but took time (usually at least 24 hours) and considerable space, and only large packing houses had refrigerated storage areas.

Hydrocooling was developed in the early 1930s. This involved either spraying produce with a refrigerated mist of water in an enclosed area or soaking the produce in cold water.

Vacuum precooling was developed in the early 1940s and became common over the next decade. This involved spraying the produce with a mist of water, then placing it in a sealed chamber and applying a light vacuum. This caused fast evaporation of the water, which cooled the produce quickly.

This could be done on a small scale, with stacks of crates placed in a small chamber or tube at the field or packing house. Large chambers in some locations allowed an entire refrigerator car or truck to be done at once.

Lettuce, various greens, melons, asparagus, celery, citrus, and carrots were often precooled by these methods.

Processing, packing, and loading

Whatever the method of harvest, fruits and vegetables arrived at packing houses by wagon or truck. Most common is in field boxes or field crates that are designed for reuse and much heavier than shipping crates. Baskets and sacks are also common. Potatoes and some other produce may arrive in bulk by truck, **17**.

Processing, packing, and shipping varies by type of fruit or vegetable, and methods can vary by different regions, shippers, packing houses, and era. The following are general summaries. We'll concentrate on the ice-bunker period.

Citrus fruit and apples

Oranges and other citrus fruit usually arrive in field boxes and were typically placed in a cooling room to remove field heat, **18**. Oranges were sometimes treated with ethylene gas by spraying under a tarp to tint them orange (if picked green). The fruit was then washed and rinsed, a wax coating applied, and then dried.

Citrus fruits and apples were sorted by hand for size and grade. The best fruit would head for direct sale to consumers; lower grades were sent to juice or other food processing facilities (the percentage of oranges processed into concentrate greatly increased in the 1950s).

A lot of oranges, apples, and grapefruit were individually wrapped in tissue before packing (this was more common in California than Florida), **19**. Wooden crates were typical through the 1950s, and then cardboard boxes were used.

Crates would be stacked in cars in a staggered pattern for airflow, often on end. A standard load for orange crates in a 40-foot reefer was 462 boxes (per PFE), and for apples, 800 boxes for an ice-bunker car. For citrus, cars were usually iced before delivery to packing sheds. For apples, it would depend upon the season and outdoor temperatures.

Potatoes and onions

Incoming potatoes could be sorted and bagged in the field or at a packing house. Spuds arriving at a packing house were dumped into a water tub or tank for cleaning and then carried up on a conveyor while being sprayed with a rinse. Sorters on the line removed bad potatoes and any stray material.

Once dry, they can be hand-graded for size, but large operations did this automatically by passing them across a screen or grate with a series of

18
Flatbed trucks deliver field boxes filled with oranges to the Redlands, Calif., Cooperative Fruit Association packing house in the early 1940s. *Library of Congress*

19
Fruit was packed by hand in crates, and citrus was often wrapped in tissue as it was packed. These oranges are also stamped Sunkist. *Library of Congress*

20

Workers pack ice in wooden crates with carrots at Elsa, Texas, in February 1939.
Russell Lee, Library of Congress

21

Ice is shaved and placed on top of spinach in baskets at an outdoor platform in Texas in 1939. The baskets are packed tightly in the ART reefer, with more ice placed on top of the load. *Library of Congress*

progressively larger slots or holes. The potatoes fall through them as they go. Potatoes travel down a chute to a bagger, with a burlap sack sitting on a scale; at 100 pounds, the sacker swaps sacks and ties off the full one.

By the early 1950s, some houses were packing spuds directly for retail sale in smaller (10- to 25-pound) paper bags, several of which are then packed into a larger bag or sack.

Refrigerator car floors were usually laid with padded paper sheets to protect bags on the bottom. Sacks are hand-trucked from loaders into reefers. A typical load for a 40-foot ice car was 360 100-pound sacks.

Potato cars were usually delivered to packing houses dry (no ice), and—depending on season—they were often moved in ventilator service. In late fall or winter, spuds would require heaters. Bangor & Aroostook had insulated boxcars with built-in heaters for this, and Northern Pacific used insulated cars with portable heaters.

Onions also were packed in sacks but were shipped at a cooler temperature—usually the low to mid 30s. Onions and potatoes both have fairly long shelf lives as long as they're stored in cool, dry environments.

Lettuce and other vegetables

Lettuce could be packed in crates in the field or at a packing house. Through the 1940s, it was common to add crushed ice among the individual heads in a crate. Other produce receiving this treatment were celery, carrots, spinach, and cabbage, **20**. Wooden crates were used, with baskets sometimes used for celery and spinach, **21**.

These products were often vacuum precooled once that technology became available, with ice no longer needed in individual baskets or crates.

Many shippers preferred to ship these products top-iced, with a layer of finely crushed ice covering the entire load, **22**. This helped keep the humidity high as well as the temperature low. Others shipped the loads with bunker ice only after precooling, while some shippers specified bunker ice plus top-icing.

In the mid-1950s, with vacuum precooling, cardboard boxes came into wide use, **23**. Carrots in crates were shipped whole (with green tops on) and often top-iced. By the late 1950s, carrots were often prepped by cutting off the top greens, packed in plastic bags (intended for retail sale), and then the bags were placed in boxes. Other vegetables also began being prepped for retail sale prior to packing.

Melons, berries, and grapes

Melons include watermelon, cantaloupe, honeydew, and other varieties, **13**. They're picked and brought to a packing house, where they're graded, sized, and crated.

Watermelons are stored and shipped at 55 to 60 degrees (warmer or cooler temps speed spoilage). This relatively high temperature range meant they were often shipped in ventilated boxcars (which were often called "melon cars") that were especially common in the East and Southeast, **24**. They could also be shipped in standard refrigerator cars, often in ventilator service. In the early 1900s, they were often shipped uncrated and stacked in cars. Crates and containers became more common after that.

Cantaloupes are very perishable. They were precooled to 35–40 degrees for shipping (vacuum cooled when available) and have a much shorter shelf life than watermelons. This means they were usually shipped with ice, and sometimes they had ice added on top of their cases. Honeydew melons were shipped in a middle range: 45–50 degrees, with a longer storage life.

Berries, cherries, grapes, and peaches are all highly perishable items, **25**. They cooled to around freezing as soon as possible after picking and held around 32 degrees to preserve them. They often were shipped in express refrigerators (strawberries were the most common produce shipped by express), **26**.

Tomatoes are another fragile perishable, but they were shipped at higher temperature (upper 50s), meaning they could often travel with ventilator service.

22 Many shippers opted for top-icing for leafy vegetables. The "slingers" would guide the finely crushed ice to each end of the car, filling the space above the crates. *Santa Fe*

23 With the advent of vacuum precooling in the 1950s, packing lettuce shifted to cardboard boxes. Here, workers load boxes aboard a PFE mechanical car near Salinas, Calif., in the 1970s. *Elrond Lawrence*

Farmers transfer watermelons from wagons to Pennsylvania Railroad ventilated boxcars at Laurel, Del., in 1905. *Library of Congress*

A federal inspector checks strawberries before loading. Berries are fragile—these are packed in small trays that are then placed inside wood crates. *Russell Lee, Library of Congress*

Strawberries were the most common produce shipped by express. Here, cases are loaded onto a National Refrigerator Car Co. wood express reefer at Hammond, La., in February 1939. *Russell Lee, Library of Congress*

These produce items were all susceptible to bruising, so they were packed securely in crates or boxes to minimize handling and touching while still allowing ventilation and airflow.

Bananas

Bananas were the most common imported fruit. They entered the United States and were directly transloaded from ship to railcar at many ports including New Orleans, San Francisco, Charleston, Baltimore, and Mobile. Most came by ship from Central America, **27**.

Through the 1950s, bananas were harvested green, with the goal to get them to their destination before allowing them to ripen. They were shipped in bunches, still attached to their main central stalks. Bananas are extremely temperature sensitive in shipment: temperatures below 56 degrees can permanently inhibit ripening, and letting them warm above 60 will cause premature ripening and possible spoilage before delivery.

Vertical conveyor belts with baskets carried bunches out of a ship's hold. The bananas were then graded, with each bunch labeled. They could then be carried on horizontal conveyors to cars or simply carried by laborers. At the railcars, they were tallied and placed vertically on the floor on their stalks, **28**. They were braced with wood strips in one layer.

The Illinois Central figured about 300 bunches/stems could be loaded in a 40-foot reefer. At about 75 pounds each, this made for an 11- to 13-ton load.

Once delivered, bananas were kept in ripening rooms where they were hung by their stalks, with the temperature regulated to control ripening. They were then cut, boxed, and shipped to final users by truck.

A disease wiped out many banana plants in the late 1950s and early 1960s, leading to new varieties being planted and grown, which changed the shipping method as well. From the early 1960s onward, bananas were packed in cardboard boxes at the growing areas. Most banana traffic shifted to trucks by the 1960s, and refrigerated containers still move this traffic today.

A conveyor brings bananas up from a ship's hold in 1910. Through the 1950s, bananas were shipped in bunches, still attached to their stalks. *Library of Congress*

Bunches of bananas are carried by hand from a ship to refrigerator cars in Mobile, Ala., in 1937. *Arthur Rothstein, Library of Congress*

1

CHAPTER FIVE

Perishable operations

A Santa Fe Alco switcher is busy delivering refrigerator cars to Kern County, Calif., packing sheds as the potato rush gears up in a late spring in the early 1950s. *Santa Fe*

Fruits and vegetables have limited shelf lives, so speed is the key to getting them to market with as much freshness remaining as possible. Into the 1960s, railroads did this by operating solid trains of reefers on expedited schedules or by operating large blocks of reefers in other priority freight trains, **1**.

The National Perishable Freight Committee issued rules and instructions for handling perishables. This 1958 Santa Fe guide is a supplement to the main publication.

U.S. refrigerator car loads by type, 1943

Perishables	Carloads
Potatoes	260,657
Vegetables, N.O.S.*	170,591
Oranges/grapefruit	150,863
Apples	42,867
Bananas	38,524
Onions	30,309
Fruits, N.O.S.**	27,076
Tomatoes	25,302
Cabbage	24,801
Watermelons	17,763
Grapes	18,687
Limes/lemons	15,960
Cantaloupes/other melons	15,119
Peaches	12,129
Tropical fruits	3,103
Berries	1,663
Nonperishables	
Canned food products	336,335
Beverages	201,005

*Not Otherwise Specified: includes lettuce, spinach, carrots, celery, and others

**Pears, plums, apricots, and others

List does not include meat or dairy products

Source: *Railway Age*, February 10, 1945

We'll look at railroad operations from the early 1900s onward, concentrating on the classic era through the 1950s and closing with a look at how perishable traffic declined and what traffic still moves by rail today.

Extensive markets

About 85 percent of fruits and vegetables are produced (or imported) south and west of Chicago, while a majority is consumed north and east of Chicago. The distance between producers and consumers means perishable traffic has always involved long hauls—the average perishable shipment was about 1,400 miles in 1941.

California is the country's major producer of fruits and vegetables, with a wide variety also coming out of Florida, Texas, and Arizona. Many other states and regions produce specialty products at various times of the year, including Maine potatoes,

Washington apples, South Carolina peaches, and Louisiana strawberries. At any given time from January to December, *something* is being harvested *somewhere*.

Under the Interstate Commerce Act, when a shipper contacted a railroad with perishable goods to transport, the railroad was required to provide refrigerator cars and provide the charges for shipping and for protective services.

As chapter 3 explains, railroads sometimes did this with their own cars but most often with cars of a contracted subsidiary or leasing company.

Protective services

A key in refrigerator car traffic is providing protective services, making sure goods are transported at the proper temperatures to keep them from spoiling. Shippers could choose from a number of options depending upon the product and season.

For ice-bunker cars, this meant a combination of precooling, icing (including initial icing and re-icing), ventilation, and heating. Instructions and rules for protective services were covered by the Perishable Protective Tariff, summarized in the National Perishable Freight Committee's Code of Rules for Handling Perishable Freight, which was updated periodically to reflect new technology and services, **2**.

It's important to understand the various terms for protective services and the options that were available to shippers with ice-bunker cars.

Icing is the process of filling a car's bunkers with ice (details can be found in chapter 6).

Pre-icing means icing the car prior to delivering the car to the shipper for loading.

Initial icing is the first icing done after the car is loaded.

Re-icing means adding ice to replenish earlier ice that has melted.

A long eastbound train of reefers in ventilator service, with hatches propped open, passes three new Alco DL-701 demonstrators. The action is on the Southern Pacific near Camarillo, Calif., in 1956. *Don Sims*

A worker lowers a charcoal heater into a reefer bunker with a pickeroon. It's winter 1943 on the Indiana Harbor Belt. *Jack Delano, Library of Congress*

This is typically done every 24 to 30 hours while a car is in transit.

Precooling means getting the refrigerator carload to the required temperature (removing field heat from produce and vegetables). This can be done by various means prior to loading, typically done at larger packing houses, but not at smaller packing sheds or where cars were loaded at harvest fields (see chapter 4).

Precooling can also be done after the load is in the car, either by portable refrigeration units or by stationary plants. With these, flexible ductwork is connected to the ice hatches. Refrigerated air is pumped through, bringing the load to the required temperature in an hour or two.

Precooling can also be done on fan-equipped cars by the use of portable precooling motors, applied after initial icing. Most produce cars built after 1940 were fan-equipped (and many earlier cars were retrofitted with them).

Stage icing was possible with many refrigerator cars. Cars so equipped had a grate that folded into place at mid-height of each bunker, allowing a half-load of ice to be added atop it.

Top-icing is adding crushed ice directly over the load inside the car itself. This was often done with lettuce, spinach, and other leafy vegetables when high humidity was desired.

Salt was often added to bunker ice. Salt makes ice melt faster, cooling the load faster and resulting in cooler temperatures. Ice alone could get a car interior close to freezing (32 degrees). Adding 10 pounds of salt per 100 pounds of ice drops the temperature to 21 degrees; 30 pounds of salt per 100 pounds of ice could, in ideal conditions, drop the temperature to -6 degrees (used for transporting frozen foods).

Ventilator service involves propping open a reefer's hatch covers to allow outside air to flow through the car, **3**. It's an efficient way of regulating interior temperature when the outside temperature is favorable. By the 1920s, most refrigerator cars (those not in meat service, which often had brine tanks instead of bunkers) could be used in ventilator service.

Heating (technically "protective service against cold") was another option. In cold weather, fruits and vegetables needed to be kept at or above their minimum transport temperatures. This was done with portable heaters that would be lowered into the bunkers, **4.** Early heaters used charcoal, but by the 1940s, alcohol-fueled heaters with thermostatic controls became common.

Heaters would be placed and removed as directed by instructions on the waybill. As a warning to workers, cars with heaters had placards applied to the hatches and doors.

Shipper options

Shippers could choose the type of protective service needed based upon the commodity being carried, the anticipated outdoor temperatures along the route, and the estimated length of transit time. Each car's waybill specified the type of protection required for its load regarding ventilation, refrigeration, and heating.

With standard refrigeration, cars were initially iced and then periodically and regularly re-iced in transit, with bunkers topped off each time. Waybills can specify precooling by either the shipper or carrier. Special refrigeration detailed the amount and number of times a car is re-iced in transit. It could also specify top-ice only or no re-icing. Shippers did this to reduce shipping costs (see Protective service costs chart above).

Depending on the product, shippers could also select standard ventilation, special ventilation, or combination ventilation service. The Code of Rules (under Rule 230-D) listed, by commodity, the specific outdoor temperature at which hatches would be opened or closed.

For example, standard ventilation for tomatoes calls for vents to be opened above 45 degrees and closed below 45 degrees. Shippers would choose this option if the anticipated temps on the route were in the 30–60 degree range. In warmer weather—if temps were in the 70s—a refrigeration option would be chosen instead.

The listing of standard ventilation took several pages and went into great detail, such as for flower bulbs:

Protective service costs

Shipper's charge for various options for ice-bunker refrigeration on a carload of apples traveling from Oregon to Jersey City, 1955	
Standard refrigeration	
(Initial ice, re-ice at each station)	$125.64
Special refrigeration	
Initial ice, no re-ice	18.52
Initial ice, re-ice once	64.80
Initial ice, re-ice twice	84.64
Initial ice, re-ice three times	97.75
Pre-iced, replenished, no re-ice	53.57
Pre-iced, replenished, re-ice once	71.42
Pre-iced, replenished, re-ice twice	91.25
Pre-iced, replenished, re-ice three times	103.50
Top-icing*	37.21

*Top-icing would not be used for apples; price is included to show cost for other commodities. Based on 6 tons at $5.83 per ton plus supervision fee.

Salt added to bunkers would be an additional charge ($.75 per 100 pounds).

Note: This is billing for the refrigeration charge only, not the total shipping rate.

Mechanical refrigeration: The refrigeration charge for this load in a mechanical car would be based on standard ice refrigeration (in this case, $125.64). A frozen shipment in a mechanical car would be billed at 1.5 times the standard refrigeration rate for fresh vegetables ($188.46).

Sources: *Railway Age*, "Perishable Demands are Exacting," April 18, 1955; *Freight Traffic Red Book*, 1955, pg. 700 (contracts for protective services)

Shipping costs: Cost of shipping one full car of plums on Santa Fe from Bakersfield to Chicago in 1953, including protective services (standard refrigeration):
Freight refrigerator: $923 standard; $1,169 expedited (Santa Fe's high-speed Train 62).
Express refrigerator: $1,214 (Railway Express Agency)

Source: *Modern Railroads*, "No. 62 Sets Freight Record," July 1953

"Keep vents closed during day and open during night, except keep vents closed when raining or at 40 degrees or lower."

Special ventilation allowed shippers to customize the service, for example, by specifying other temperatures for opening or closing vents or by specifying locations ("keep vents closed to [station]; keep vents open thereafter").

Combination ventilation combines standard and special, usually by specifying standard ventilation to a certain location and then special ventilation thereafter.

Shippers paid both a shipping charge for the load as well as a fee for refrigeration. Charges for mechanical cars were based on fees for ice-bunker cars.

Privately owned reefers weren't subject to the per diem rules of standard freight cars (in which a railroad paid a fee—$1 in 1943 and $2 in 1955—to the owner of each car

on its railroad at midnight each day). Instead, railroads paid reefer owners a mileage charge—2 cents a mile in 1943 and 4 cents in 1955—for both loaded and empty movements.

Car delivery

The first step in the process was for the shipper (local packing shed or grower, large packing house, co-op, or preparation plant) to call an agent at the servicing railroad and request cars. This would be done at least a day in advance. Shippers would also alert agents to potential future needs.

Orders ranged from a single car or two to be placed on a spur or siding next to a harvest area to dozens of cars placed at a large packing house in peak season. The local agent will have cars delivered as needed with the shipper's requested protective services directed on each waybill. Shippers could request cars "dry" (without ice) or pre-iced.

The car supplier, as chapter 4 explains, could be the railroad itself,

5 Several ART refrigerator cars have been dropped off for potato loading at Monte Vista, Colo., on the Denver & Rio Grande Western in October 1939. *Arthur Rothstein, Library of Congress*

a leasing company, or a contracted subsidiary. A packing house on the Southern Pacific would call the SP, which used subsidiary Pacific Fruit Express to supply the cars. A nearby packing house on the Santa Fe would call that railroad, with the Santa Fe Refrigerator Department (SFRD) providing the cars and protective services. In Washington, an apple packer on the Great Northern would receive Western Fruit Express cars (or from another member of that group, such as Fruit Growers Express).

Car distributors working for the car owner (PFE or SFRD) would have already been working to track incoming cars, making sure they're stockpiled in regions where they will be needed.

Car owners track cars returning from trips, tally how many are cleaned and ready for a new shipment, and direct them to the regions or areas where they're needed. Owners know the peak growing seasons and have a rough idea in advance of how many cars will be needed to cover shipments.

A PFE car returning from New York City, where it had just delivered a load of Texas vegetables, might be cleaned and next routed to California.

Depending upon the crop and season, multiple shippers in one area could request hundreds of cars at the same time. This could tax the car fleets of even major operations such as PFE, SFRD, or FGE. At peak times, many car owners would lease or otherwise share available cars. This means cars of Merchants Despatch (MDT), FGE, or American Refrigerator Transit (ART) might occasionally appear at PFE-served packing houses on the SP, or a PFE reefer might show up at an FGE-served citrus plant in Florida. Some owners did not share, for example PFE and SFRD.

Clean, empty cars would be stored on assigned yard tracks or nearby spurs or sidings. Switchers would bring cars to icing docks as needed (to fill orders for pre-iced cars) and then local freights would bring the dry and pre-iced cars to packing houses and loading areas, **5**. During busy seasons,

local freights would be supplanted with dedicated switching jobs or extra trains to handle the increased traffic.

For the most part, empties would be spotted in the evening or overnight so they were ready for loading the following morning. Loaded cars would be picked up in the afternoon or evening, **6**. At peak times, local freights or dedicated switching jobs could pull loaded cars and set out new empties once or twice per day.

The exact process varied by railroad and specific locale, but local trains received information from the local depot agent or from the individual shipper regarding where cars should be spotted.

Precooling and preparation

When loaded cars were picked up, how they were handled varied. Shippers that loaded goods that were not precooled generally used dry (non-iced) cars. These cars would be switched to a nearby precooling plant, or would be taken to a platform, iced,

A Santa Fe local freight extra has just picked up loads from the packing sheds near Bakersfield, Calif., in October 1940. The 4-6-2 has eight SFRD reefers and a caboose. *R. H. Kindig*

and precooled by having exterior motors applied to power the cars' fans to precool the loads. Once the cars were precooled, the ice would be topped off and the cars would be brought to the proper yard and consolidated for movement by outbound trains.

Cars with precooled loads were usually ordered pre-iced. These cars would be taken to the ice dock to be topped off and then brought to the yard ready to roll.

A shipper may waybill a car directly to a specific customer, such as a wholesaler or supermarket chain. However, because market prices for perishables can vary greatly by location (and from day to day), shippers often either sent cars on their way east and sold them en route or diverted them, changing the final destination (which could happen multiple times for any given car). These cars were called "rollers" or "diversions."

Railroads provided for this service in billing and handling, allowing waybills to be changed three times without an additional charge. During peak seasons, more than half the cars were rollers. Agents tracked rollers, transmitting information by telegraph and then later by teletype and telephone, with reports provided to shippers.

Rollers were an efficient way to keep cars moving. They allowed shippers to load and send cars right away, instead of letting them sit while speculating about market needs and prices. It was a self-correcting process to get cars to markets where they were most needed and desired.

Even with complete trains of reefers, these were not unit trains, as each car had its own waybill, and cars in a given train might be bound for dozens of final destinations, **7**.

Basic train operations

The main goal of perishable operations, especially for railroads that operated a lot of cars over long distances, was speed. This was complicated by the necessity to pause to re-ice and inspect cars on a regular basis, as well as to switch cars in or out of trains as needed.

By the 1930s, standard freight service from California to Chicago took 9 or 10 days, with a total of 12–14 days to New York City. Dedicated perishable trains on expedited schedules could get reefers to Chicago in about 7 days and New York in 10 or 11 days. By the 1950s, improved equipment, better insulated cars, and diesel power allowed 4-day service to Chicago and 7- or 8-day

service to New York. Mechanical reefer service from PFE by the 1970s had refrigerator cars moving from California to New York in 6 days.

In the East, trains running north from Florida to New York and Philadelphia promised delivery on the fifth morning at each city through the 1920s. By 1930, railroads had trimmed this to the fourth morning.

Train size was limited by number of cars and total tonnage. Loaded reefers are lighter than other freight cars (a load of 12–18 tons per car was common, plus ice), which allowed for longer trains. Tonnage ratings depended upon locomotives and grades, with many railroads having helper districts. Improved car design, better brakes, and longer icing platforms made longer trains more practical and efficient.

Through the 1930s, limits of 50–60 cars were common, but by the late 1940s, many railroads were running 100-car trains weighing 4,000–5,000 tons.

Other than passenger trains (First Class in the timetable), perishable trains were generally the hottest trains on a railroad. Many railroads gave them Second Class timetable status. They could also be operated as Extras, allowing dispatchers to weave them among other trains using train orders.

Western Pacific Fruit Block 344

The Western Pacific carried perishables from northern California destined for eastern markets, often in full trains. Fruit Block 344 (officially Train 62) was one such train in the late fall of 1951. The WP didn't haul the volume of traffic as neighbors SP, Santa Fe, or UP, but still ran 1–6 such "supermarket" trains a day depending upon the season (about 17,000 perishable carloads a year).

Trains were assembled at either Stockton or Sacramento, destined for the WP's eastern terminus at Salt Lake City. There cars continued their journeys via connections with UP and Rio Grande.

Train makeup, and the contents of the reefers, depended upon the growing season and train's originating point. Our WP train departing Stockton, Calif., on a late fall day in 1951 had 56 reefers: 42 cars of celery, 6 cars of tomatoes, 4 cars of black grapes, 2 cars of carrots, 1 car of lettuce, and 1 car of dressed turkeys. The train also carried 14 cars of dead freight (nonperishable freight) as fill, for a total of 70 cars.

The WP blocked the train based on destination and connections: reefers for UP behind the locomotive, followed by reefers for D&RGW, UP dead freight, D&RGW dead freight, and then cars to be set out before Salt Lake at the end.

The train left Stockton at 7:15 p.m. behind a 4-unit set of EMD FTs and was due at Salt Lake City late on the second morning of its trip: 39½ hours to cover 838 miles. (Sacramento trains were scheduled for 36 hours, 40 minutes).

At 10:35 p.m., the train arrived in Oroville, Calif., the first crew-change point, where another reefer (mixed celery and carrots) was cut in. The train rolled through the night, arriving at Portola, Calif., at 6:15 a.m., where the cars were iced and a switcher added 16 dead-freight cars of fill.

The train continued without change in consist through the day, arriving in Elko, Nev., at 6:55 p.m. There, a switcher pulled off 18 cars of dead freight and added 13 empty stock cars, which were dropped off several miles later at Tobar, in time for a priority cattle loading assignment.

An A-B-B-A set of Electro-Motive FT diesels leads an eastbound Fruit Block train on Western Pacific in the 1940s, bound for Salt Lake City. *Western Pacific*

During the summer (April 16 to September 30, per WP instructions), eastbound perishable trains stop at Carlin, Nev. (just west of Elko) for regular icing. Once the cold weather of October hits—as with our train—Carlin reverts to being an emergency icing station only, with eastbounds continuing to Salt Lake City before re-icing.

At Shafter, Nev., the WP meets the Nevada Northern. Because there was no local freight operating that day and the Fruit Block was running ahead of schedule, it was given the duty of stopping at the interchange to pick up 9 loads of copper ingots and 29 empty cars. The empties were removed 2 hours later at Wendover, Utah, with the loads continuing to Salt Lake.

Fruit Block 344 rolled into Roper Yard at Salt Lake City at 8:30 a.m., 90 minutes ahead of schedule, and the blocks of reefers were shortly iced and on their way to their UP and Rio Grande connections with time to spare.

Waybills and icing

The train's varied lading (sample cars at right) meant icing crews treated individual cars differently, following the waybill instructions. An example: tomato cars labeled SV (standard ventilation) began their journey with hatches open in the 50-degree weather around Sacramento. However, because of freezing temperatures east of Oroville, these cars had their hatches closed at Oroville.

PFE 41320—Lettuce (427 crates of assorted lettuce and parsley), bound for Chicago. Routing: WP/D&RGW/MoPac/ Wabash. Its waybill read: "Dry car loaded: keep plugs in vents. Top-iced by shipper at origin with 15,000#, rule 242." On the train list, this was summarized as VC (vents closed), which would let all train and icing crews know that the car was not to be opened or iced while in transit.

PFE 65400—Celery, billed to A&P stores in Scranton, Pa. Routing: WP/UP/ MILW/NKP/DL&W/D&H. Waybill: "Dry car loaded. Initial ice to capy. at Stockton. Do not re-ice (Rule 240). 15,000# top ice supplied by shipper at terminus (Rule 242). On train list: DNR (do not re-ice).

PFE 64550—Wine grapes, bound for Jersey City, N. J. Routing: (car had come to WP off subsidiary Tidewater Southern) WP/UP/CNW/Erie. Waybill: "Pre-iced car furnished. Re-ice to full capacity all regular icing stations. Supply 2% salt Stockton based on bunker capacity, 1% salt at Portola based on amount of salt supplied; No further salt." Train list: SR1% (salt re-ice 1 percent).

PFE 60139—Tomatoes, bound for Kansas City. Routing: WP/D&RGW/ CB&Q. Waybill: "Dry car ordered and loaded. Close vents at 45 degrees; open vents above 45 degrees. Tomatoes Section 7 no recourse." Train list: SV (standard ventilation).

Information taken from "The Log of Fruit Block 344," by W. H. Hutchinson, published in *Trains & Travel*, August 1952.

7 Santa Fe refrigerator cars loaded with potatoes from Kern County, Calif., head eastward at Topock, Ariz., in 1953. Even though it's a solid train of one commodity, the cars have many different destinations. *Santa Fe*

OVERLAND ROUTE

Note A OS	Note B R	Note C OVE	Note D SV	Note E NWP	Note F TBXE	Note G SJR	Note I SME	Miles	
		11 00	(From Coast Route)		3 00¹			0	PT San Francisco PT
		11 40			4 00¹			21	Redwood Jct.
			6 00¹			12 01¹		—	San Jose
		2 40¹ 3 15¹				3 00¹ 3 45¹		79	Tracy
		5 50¹	11 59¹	Schellville		6 20¹		140	Polk
		3 30¹	8 00¹	5 00¹	7 00¹		11 15	0	Oakland
	(Conns. Lodi-NWP-SV "F" Blocks)	6 30¹	11 30¹	7 00¹			2 15¹	87	Sacramento
		7 30¹	12 45¹	8 00¹			3 00¹	105	Roseville
	10 00¹	6 30¹ 3 00¹ (Conn. "R" Block)	12 45¹ (Conn. "R" Block)			7 00¹ (To Shasta Route)		159	Roseville
(From Shasta Route) 9 00¹	5 00¹ 5 30¹	10 30¹ 11 00¹						296	Sparks
								326	Fernley
12 01⁴	1 30²	9 00²						579	Carlin
3 00⁴	10 50²	9 00²						827	PT Ogden PT
	Via DRGW	Via UP						827	MT Ogden MT
	3 50²	1 15²							
								1310	MT Cheyenne MT
	11 59³	12 01⁴						1404	MT Denver MT
		7 30⁴ 11 00⁴						1536	MT CT North Platte MT CT
		7 50⁴ 9 50⁴						1820	CT Council Bluffs CT
		8 30⁴						1934	Kansas City
		8 00⁴						2206	St. Louis
	9 30²	11 30⁴						2293	CT Chicago CT

A—OS (Oregon Special) originates at Eugene (see Shasta Route) and operates to Ogden with both perishable and manifest traffic.

B—R (Roseville Blocks) operated for eastward perishable freight traffic concentrated at Roseville. Cut-off time for delivery of perishable to U.P. is 11:50 p.m., M.T., (on arrival), and to D.R.G.W. 3:50 a.m., M.T.

C—OVE (Overland East) handles traffic from San Francisco for Tracy and beyond, and from Oakland to Roseville and beyond. Traffic from San Francisco for San Joaquin Valley connects with AE at Tracy. Traffic from San Francisco for Shasta Route connects with RPS and KFX at Roseville.

D—SV (Salinas Vegetable Block) originates Watsonville Junction (see Coast Route). Connects with Roseville Blocks at Roseville for movement eastward on first day. Perishable for Pacific Northwest connects with NCP from Roseville second day (see Shasta Route).

E—NWP (Northwestern Pacific Perishable) is due from Northwestern Pacific Schellville 5:00 a.m. Connects with Roseville Blocks from Roseville on the same day.

F—TBXE (Trans-Bay Extra) operates from San Francisco to Oakland with local perishable and manifest traffic.

G—SJR (San Jose-Roseville Extra) handles traffic for Tracy and beyond. Traffic for San Joaquin Valley connects with AE at Tracy. Traffic for Shasta Route connects with RPS and KFX at Roseville. Traffic for Overland Route connects with OVE at Roseville.

I—SME (Shasta Manifest East) from Oakland handles available manifest traffic for Shasta Route. Picks up Shasta Route and Overland Route traffic at Port Costa. Also handles merchandise cars from Oakland for Sacramento, Reno and Ogden and beyond.

8 This timetable is from Southern Pacific's "Condensed Perishable, Merchandise, and Manifest Train Schedule No. 18" from March 1959. It shows eastbound trains only. Light numbers are a.m., dark numbers are p.m., and superscript numbers indicate the day in transit.

It was rare for a train to start and finish its journey with the same consist of cars. If possible, an originating yard would dispatch a solid train of reefers up to its car or tonnage limit. Additional reefers would often be picked up at junctions (foreign or home road) and division points, and reefers would be set out for connecting trains and railroads as well.

An eastbound Union Pacific train of 70 cars arriving at North Platte, Neb., might have 25 cars pulled for Kansas City connections, another 10 bound for Minneapolis and northern connections that will be switched out at Omaha, with the remaining 35 continuing on to Chicago (including eastern connections).

Unless heading to Chicago or New York, cars tended to gradually disperse, soon traveling in blocks, and then often as single cars in way freights to final customers in smaller areas. Plenty of cars ended their journeys not at major produce yards but alone at the dock of a food wholesaler in a small city, dropped off by a local freight.

A perishable train may carry other "hot" cars, typically meat reefers, stock cars, auto parts cars, or other scheduled cars such as merchandise (LCL, less-than-carload) boxcars.

Trains may also have lower priority cars of "dead freight" (nonperishable loads) added, called "fill," generally with these guidelines: dead freight traveled at the end of the train, dead freight couldn't slow train operation (especially important in mountain territory), dead freight would only be set out or picked up at regular icing stops (the rear end can be switched while reefers are iced) or yards where reefers would also be switched, and dead freight would be removed en route if new priority cars were added.

Railroads published timetables and instructions listing the cars/traffic carried by each train. An example taken from a Southern Pacific San Francisco to Chicago shippers' timetable in 1959 is shown in figure **8**.

If there weren't enough perishable cars to operate as a separate train, loaded reefers would be carried in a priority freight train. They almost always traveled at the front of a train in a solid block to make it easier to ice cars and switch them out at their terminal.

Railroads blocked trains—arranged cars in groups by destination—as much as possible. This made both en route and terminal switching easier and faster. For example, the Western Pacific train described on page 72 had two blocks of reefers, one each for its Union Pacific and Rio Grande connections at Salt Lake City.

Railroads devoted significant space in yards for classifying perishable traffic—often adjacent to icing facilities. An example was Kansas City on the Union Pacific, which dedicated 16 yard tracks for perishables. The UP classified 30,000 cars here in 1953 (7,800 in the peak month of July). It was a key point with many cars heading to multiple destinations and other railroads, likewise empty PFE reefers returning from foreign roads.

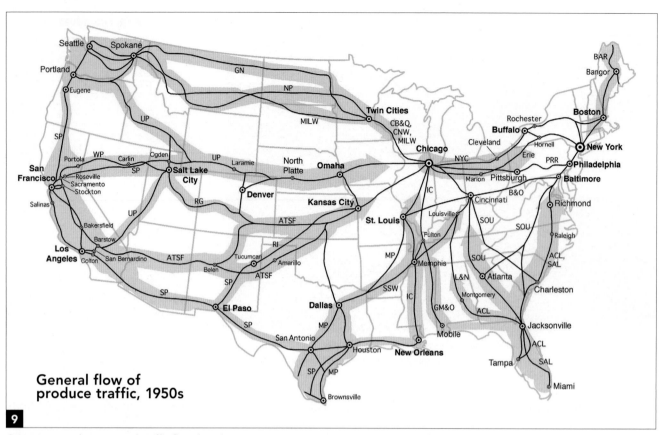

General flow of produce traffic, 1950s

9

Orange areas show general traffic flow, but they are not meant to represent specific traffic volumes. All railroads and cities not shown.

Although most perishable traffic was heading east or north, there were westbound loads as well. They were generally not numerous enough to warrant their own trains but could be found as individual cars or blocks. They could be difficult to spot among the sea of empties returning west, but they would require stopping at icing platforms en route.

California routes and railroads

California has long been the country's major source of fruits and vegetables. The state stretches almost 800 miles from north to south, and at more than 160,000 square miles, California is three times the size of New York—and is blessed with many fertile growing areas.

It follows that California loaded more refrigerator cars than any other region. In the peak years of perishable traffic, California annually shipped more than 50,000 carloads of citrus fruit, 50,000 cars of lettuce, and 30,000 cars of potatoes, not to mention thousands of cars of other fruits and vegetables and frozen goods. Peak shipping season was summer (roughly

June through October), but there wasn't a month of the year that something wasn't being harvested and shipped in the state.

This traffic headed eastward on four railroads. The Santa Fe, Union Pacific, and Southern Pacific sent trains out of southern California; Southern Pacific and Western Pacific in the north; and Southern Pacific and Santa Fe both had lines running through central California growing areas, **9**.

In the south, the SP and UP consolidated cars at Colton and Santa Fe at San Bernardino. In central California, Santa Fe assembled cars at Bakersfield and SP at Salinas, and in the north, the SP sent trains out of Roseville and the WP from Stockton and Sacramento.

The primary destination for all lines was Chicago—from there, many headed to New York, while others were diverted at Kansas City, Omaha, and St. Louis for routing to other midwest or southeast destinations.

The Santa Fe's main line continued to Chicago via Arizona, New Mexico, and Texas, and then up through Kansas

City. The northern SP line met the Union Pacific at Ogden, Utah (the transcontinental Overland Route), and the WP hooked up with the UP just south of Ogden at Salt Lake City. The UP's southern line headed northeast, also linking with the Overland Route at Ogden. From Ogden, the UP carried most of this traffic eastward to Omaha, handing off to the Chicago & North Western and other railroads for Chicago. The SP's southern line (the Golden State Route) carried cars eastward with connections to Kansas City, St. Louis, and other eastern and midwestern markets.

By the 1930s, all of these routes offered seventh morning delivery in Chicago (about 146 hours). By the 1950s, this had been reduced to four days (107 hours). Each railroad had names or terms for their perishable trains: Santa Fe called its trains GFX (Green Fruit Express); SP and UP had Colton and Roseville Perishable Blocks (C or CPB, R or RPB), Salinas Vegetable Block (SV), and other symbols by originating station, and the WP had Fruit Blocks.

Illinois Central Train 52, a Banana Express, is northbound with 34 loaded cars in ventilator service near Wetaug, Ill., in May 1903.
C. W. Witbeck collection

During peak seasons, the Santa Fe might run 9 or 10 solid trains of reefers daily to Chicago; the SP and UP might run an additional 6–8 each, with the WP adding 3–6. This volume meant scheduling was important, making sure trains were spaced properly to avoid congestion at icing stations and intermediate and terminal yards, and that connection times were met at handoff points with other railroads.

Florida and the Southeast
Florida had become a major producer of citrus fruits, melons, and various vegetables by the 1910s. In the 1919–20 citrus season, Florida produced 39 percent of the total U.S. output, and in 1932–33, the state overtook California as the top citrus producer with 46 percent of the U.S. total.

Although best known for its oranges and grapefruit, Florida also grows other perishable crops, namely tomatoes, watermelons, green beans, and peppers. In 1921, Florida railroads moved 60,000 carloads of perishables, including 33,000 loads of citrus.

As with California products, the main markets for Florida were New York, Chicago, and other midwestern and northeastern cities. Through the 1920s, most train schedules provided delivery in New York City and Philadelphia on the fifth morning, and by 1930, this had tightened to fourth morning delivery. This meant most through trains originated in the evening, with cutoff times of 5 p.m. in south Florida and 9 p.m. in Jacksonville in the north.

The Atlantic Coast Line was Florida's main originating line for produce (47 percent in the 1940s), followed by Seaboard Air Line (36 percent) and Florida East Coast (17 percent). Almost all of these carloads (97 percent) were handed off to other railroads to complete their journeys.

For traffic to the Northeast, ACL and SAL both ran priority trains from points in Florida, consolidating them in the north and operating them through to Richmond, Va., to the Richmond, Fredericksburg & Potomac. The RF&P then took over, handing

off to the Pennsylvania Railroad at Potomac Yard (Washington, D.C.) for northern destinations.

An example was SAL's Perishable Express, Train 80, which originated in the evening in Tampa and Miami (as Train 180). The two sections were joined at Baldwin, Fla., in the morning and headed north, reaching Raleigh, N.C., the following morning and Richmond that evening.

Cars heading to midwestern and western markets followed a variety of routes, usually to Montgomery, Ala. (connections with Louisville & Nashville and Gulf, Mobile & Ohio), to Columbus, Ga. (Central of Georgia), or on the Southern to Atlanta, St. Louis, and Cincinnati, and then Chicago.

Peaches from the Carolinas and Georgia were another key seasonal item. The traffic warranted a special train, MD-22, originating on the ACL and handing off to the RF&P and then the PRR. It ran in season (May-June in Georgia, June-August in North Carolina, and July-August in South Carolina).

Frozen foods

The emergence of the frozen food market in the 1930s (see chapter 1) required new methods for transporting these goods. Freezing gave products longer shelf life than fresh products, and it led to the trend of processing and packaging store-ready products close to the growing areas.

Frozen food companies began producing packaged fish and meat, along with fruits and vegetables. As more households began replacing iceboxes with refrigerators that could store frozen food, the variety of frozen foods increased in variety and complexity. Frozen juice production in Florida jumped dramatically from 1.9 million gallons in the 1947–48 season to 10.2 million gallons a year later.

Initial frozen food producers were based in California, which led western operators SFRD and PFE to begin building so-called "super-insulated" refrigerator cars (see chapter 2), 50-foot ice-bunker cars with extra-thick insulation.

A key with frozen foods is storing and transporting them at below-zero temperatures. Anything above zero reduces shelf life. Adding 30 percent salt to the ice would, ideally, get ice-bunker car interiors a few degrees below zero.

Shippers ordered cars in advance so railroads could precool them—icing them with 30 percent salt from 12 to 36 hours before loading. After loading, cars would be picked up by local freights, re-iced (again with 30 percent salt), and brought to a yard. They were usually shipped in the same trains as other perishables, with waybill instructions specifying 30 percent salt at each re-icing.

The frozen food industry was the driving force in the development of mechanically refrigerated cars in the 1950s. Railroads began investing heavily in these cars in the 1960s and continue to carry some frozen traffic today.

However, the bulk of frozen foods went to trucks. By the mid-1950s, trucks handled about 90 percent of prepared frozen foods. Railroads fared better with frozen juice, carrying about 80 percent of Florida production in the late 1940s and 60 percent by the mid-1950s.

By the 1960s, less citrus was moving to market in fresh form. In 1944, about 17 percent of the country's total orange crop was processed (mainly canned), and by 1954, 54 percent was processed—mainly as frozen concentrates.

Frozen food traffic led to the development of the mechanical refrigerator. Here, cases of frozen orange juice are loaded aboard an early Santa Fe mechanical car. *Santa Fe*

Frozen juice production (thousands of gallons)

Season	Florida	California	Total
1947-48	1,910	590	2,500
1948-49	10,233	1,963	12,196
1949-50	24,535	5,283	29,818
1950-51	31,191	7,822	39,013
1951-52	45,100	9,650	54,750
1952-53	48,500	14,713	63,213
1953-54*	65,531	2,000	67,000
1954-55	70,850	12,300	83,150

Includes orange (California and Florida), lemon (California), and grapefruit (Florida) juices.
*Lemon and grapefruit data missing
Source: *Railway Age*, April 18, 1955

Other traffic from the region included melons from Mississippi and Georgia, sweet potatoes from Mississippi and the Carolinas, and Alabama peaches and tomatoes. Bananas were imported by the Southern at Charleston, S.C., and the GM&O at Mobile.

Fruit Growers Express supplied refrigerator cars and handled protective services (including icing stations throughout the region) for most railroads in the area, although some railroads operated their own ventilated boxcars for carrying melons (ACL, SAL, CofG, and L&N). Merchants Despatch at times supplied cars for GM&O and the Frisco.

As with California, Florida saw traffic begin shifting to trucks starting in the 1940s. In the 1940–41 season, 57 percent of Florida perishables were shipped by rail and 29 percent by truck. Totals that season were 89,000 cars of fruit and 12,000 of vegetables.

Another change in Florida was the move to frozen concentrated orange juice (FCOJ), as seen in sidebar chart above. This started small in the late 1940s, but by the mid-1950s, almost half of Florida oranges were processed as FCOJ. This meant fewer cars of fresh oranges and led to FGE's substantial fleet of mechanical cars for handling frozen products.

As with California, many cars from the Southeast were shipped as rollers. Shippers had less time for diversions than those in California, but about half of Florida carloads were shipped this way through the 1940s.

Bananas

The Illinois Central became known for its banana traffic from the port of New Orleans, which it handled from the 1890s through the 1960s, **10**. The railroad's peak year was 1947, when it handled 52,000 carloads of bananas (including some handled via interchange from the Gulf, Mobile & Ohio, which loaded them at Mobile). By comparison, PFE carried about 12,000 carloads of bananas annually from San Francisco.

The IC had a yard at Stuyvesant Docks in New Orleans. Inbound reefers were cleaned and prepped at Stuyvesant. Cars were pre-iced and delivered to various dock tracks for loading or to the New Orleans Public Belt, which switched some docks.

It took 4–8 hours to unload a ship, depending upon its size. Each ship carried enough bananas for 90–200 refrigerator cars. Cars were loaded until the ship's holds were empty. This required switch crews to continually pull loaded cars and replace them with empties. Loaded cars were pulled back to Stuyvesant, where they were weighed, re-iced, and assembled into trains.

Bananas made for a light load: just 10 or 11 tons per car (plus ice). By the 1930s, the IC generally handled them in trains of 80 to 100 cars, sending trains northward as they were assembled. Trains were scheduled to reach Chicago in just under two days (about 40 hours).

Although some cars might be set out sooner, trains generally traveled intact to Fulton, Ky., just past the halfway point to Chicago. Fulton had a 2,700-foot ice dock with a track on each side, which allowed 60–70 cars to be iced on each side at once. A connection with the GM&O just south of Fulton at Rives, Tenn., provided additional banana cars (and other southeast perishables), sometimes in solid trains.

Rio Grande Valley carloadings

Carloads of select commodities shipped on Missouri Pacific and Southern Pacific lines (including subsidiaries) from the Rio Grande Valley region in Texas:

	1930-31	1935-36	1940-41	1945-46
Cabbage MP	6,050	5,144	2,314	3,006
Cabbage SP	1,810	1,264	707	874
Potatoes MP	1,753	713	1,450	2,178
Potatoes SP	540	302	87	29
Onions MP	3,421	3,951	1,618	4,858
Onions SP	7	1	—	80
Carrots MP	850	526	1,216	2,793
Carrots SP	254	314	214	678
Beets MP	1,128	506	614	417
Beets SP	188	173	170	113
Beets/Carrots MP	547	145	262	137
Beets/Carrots SP	—	187	222	—
Spinach MP	6,357	4,009	1,229	1,398
Spinach SP	50	325	95	14
Sweet corn MP	806	234	334	1,120
Sweet corn SP	44	12	127	398
Tomatoes MP	3,400	2,379	2,754	9,140
Tomatoes SP	678	357	411	2,348
Misc. Veg. MP	6,723	6,538	6,180	9,644
Misc. Veg. SP	1,360	1,575	2,398	3,342
Grapefruit MP	1,924	2,792	6,823	16,545
Oranges MP	101	258	612	2,499
Mixed Citrus MP	202	409	518	3,302
Citrus SP	353	1,157	1,776	6,183
Watermelons MP	1,487	292	233	2,139
Total MP*	35,563	28,382	26,444	59,899
Total SP*	5,459	5,624	6,288	34,250
Total region*	41,022	34,006	32,732	94,149

*All individual commodities not shown; totals reflect all commodities.

Source: *Fruit and Vegetable Loading from Territory Served by Missouri Pacific Lines in Texas, Season 1947-48* (Missouri Pacific)

At Fulton, cars were re-iced and reblocked. Cars bound for New York and the Northeast would head up the IC's line to Louisville and continue on the Baltimore & Ohio. Cars heading west could head to St. Louis or go west on IC's Iowa line. Most cars would head north to Chicago, with some heading farther north and west (including Canada).

Upon arrival at Chicago, cars were iced at Markham Yard and forwarded to connecting railroads or to wholesale or auction yards.

As with eastern and western perishable cars, most banana cars started out as rollers, with owners selling cars and rerouting them while in transit.

Fruit company representatives kept a close eye on banana temperatures. The fruit moved in all seasons, and the trip from New Orleans to Chicago or New York could mean a dramatic difference in weather and outdoor temperature. Cars would travel using ice, ventilators, or heaters as needed.

When heaters were employed, they generally stayed with cars until delivered (unlike other produce cars). The IC heaters each had its own waybill, and other railroads returned them via railroad LCL service.

Rio Grande Valley

Although not as abundant as California or Florida, the Rio Grande Valley area of south Texas produced a lot of

Workers load spinach into ART reefers at LaPryor, Texas, in 1939, chopping ice to add to baskets. The Rio Grande Valley of Texas produced many perishables. *Russell Lee, Library of Congress*

fruits and vegetables. The area's main growing seasons were October to June, with individual products including grapefruit, onions, spinach, cabbage, and carrots (see chart on page 77).

The Missouri Pacific (on its Gulf Coast Lines and International-Great Northern subsidiary) hauled the majority of this perishable traffic out of this area, but the Southern Pacific (including subsidiary St. Louis Southwestern) also carried substantial carloads, **11**. In the 1945–46 season, the split was 59,900 carloads on MP and 34,200 for SP (plus another 1,050 express shipments).

Protective service on MoPac was provided by American Refrigerator Transit, with PFE on the SP lines. Most of this traffic moved north to St. Louis and then via many connections on other railroads to Chicago, New York, and other destinations.

Other regions and traffic

Many other areas of the country saw significant perishable traffic. Maine produced 50,000 carloads of potatoes in 1934, most originating on the Bangor & Aroostook. Some of this traffic went directly to ships at Searsport, Maine. The rest was interchanged to Maine Central (and to Boston and New York

on the New Haven) or to Canadian National or Canadian Pacific, most for New York and eastern markets. Maine spuds were shipped from late fall through winter. The BAR was known for its red, white, and blue insulated/heated cars and for trading cars with PFE between seasons.

Traffic remained substantial through the 1950s but gradually moved to trucks, and a disastrous season in 1969—exacerbated by poor service on New Haven successor Penn Central—ended the traffic.

Other significant potato regions included Idaho and North Dakota/Minnesota (Red River Valley), served by Northern Pacific, Great Northern, and Milwaukee Road. Both regions shipped mainly in fall. Idaho alone accounted for 30,000 potato loads in 1934 and 66,000 in 1951.

The apple season in Washington and Oregon produced significant traffic, especially for GN, UP, and NP. In 1920, Washington produced 27,100 carloads and Oregon another 5,400. Great Northern carried about 15,000 loads per season in the 1940s.

On GN, cars were prepped and gathered at Appleyard in Wenatchee, Wash., with trains running from September through October. Trains

were sent eastward in 100- to 110-car trains or large blocks in priority freights. Trains made it to the Twin Cities in 140 hours (6 days) by the 1930s, and by 1940, they covered the distance in 109 hours (4½ days).

Many railroads hauled a great deal of perishable traffic that they didn't originate. This was true for several railroads operating from Chicago to New York as well as along the Eastern Seaboard from Florida and the Southeast. Major carriers included Erie (see the sidebar on page 79 on Erie Train 98), Baltimore & Ohio, Pennsylvania, and New York Central.

The challenge for these lines was collecting cars from multiple railroads at originating points and scheduling pickups with other lines en route. For example, in one day at Chicago, the Erie could get multiple carloads of California produce in PFE and ATSF reefers, apples in WFE reefers from GN, Idaho potatoes from NP (both via CB&Q), and meat reefers from a half-dozen packing companies, all destined for New York.

Some railroads operated run-through perishable trains with each other, notably Pennsylvania with RF&P, ACL, and SAL from Florida, Georgia, and the Carolinas.

Erie Train 98

The Erie was a major connecting railroad in moving perishables from the Midwest to New York City and surrounding areas—it brought 30,000 carloads of fruits and vegetables into its New York terminal every year through the 1950s.

During that time, Train 98 was Erie's high-priority train dedicated to this perishable traffic. It departed Chicago in the evening and arrived in Jersey City on the second following afternoon. It picked up refrigerator cars of fruits and vegetables from most western carriers at Chicago, along with meat cars from several packing companies.

All cars beginning the journey at Chicago were not destined for New York City. Many were rollers, meaning they could still be diverted at various points. Many were already consigned to buyers in other nearby cities or would be handed off by Erie to other railroads en route.

Train 98 exchanged cars with several other carriers at interchanges along the way—10 recognized connections with foreign-road train arrival times scheduled to meet 98. There were also 5 connections with other Erie lines that crossed or met the Chicago-New York main line. Common destinations included Boston, Baltimore, Buffalo, Pittsburgh, Providence, Youngstown, and many smaller cities.

Here's an idea of how the train operated, based on schedules and instructions from the railroad in 1950.

The train is due out of Chicago at 7:30 p.m., picking up refrigerator cars from western connections, including Santa Fe, Union Pacific (via Chicago & North Western and other lines), and Burlington (including cars from Great Northern and Northern Pacific). At Loomis Street Yard, which had a receiving cutoff time of 5 p.m., 98 picked up packing house reefers. After picking up connecting cars from Belt Ry. of Chicago at Clearing Yard (6 p.m. cutoff, 7:30 p.m. departure), No. 98 arrives at Hammond, Ind., acquiring more cars from the Indiana Harbor Belt connection. At Hammond, switch engines fully assemble the train, blocking cars based on their final destinations. The train departs Hammond at 9:30 p.m.

The train will be divided into multiple sections en route: NY-98 to New York City, RC-98 to Rochester, and NE-98 to New England. If traffic warrants (generally more than 100 cars), the train will depart Hammond in multiple sections based on final destinations; otherwise, the sections will be divided at Marion, Ohio.

At Huntington, Ind., more reefers are often added via interchange with the

A hotshot Erie train pauses to ice cars at Marion, Ohio. Crews add crushed ice to a Wilson meat car as two PFE reefers of produce wait at right. *Erie Railroad*

Wabash—likely American Refrigerator Transit cars carrying fruits and vegetables from the Rio Grande Valley in Texas and other southwest points. No. 98 heads out of Huntington at 2 a.m., picking up more cars at Lima, Ohio, from the Nickel Plate before arriving at Marion, Ohio, at 6:30 a.m.

At Marion, more cars arrive from the Chesapeake & Ohio and from Erie's line to Cincinnati and Dayton (Train DN-98). Here, cars are re-iced, with diversions and cars bound for connections switched out. The train is reblocked and divided into its New England and New York sections, with NE-98 leaving at 9 a.m. and NY-98 at 10 a.m.

More cars are added and removed at Kent, Ohio (Wheeling & Lake Erie) and Sharon, Pa. (Pittsburgh & Lake Erie). Arriving at Meadville, Pa., at 3:55 p.m., NE-98 drops off any cars bound for Rochester, Buffalo, and other connections. These cars will become Train RC-98 (due out of Meadville at 6:45 p.m.). Just east of Jamestown, N.Y., RC-98 will head up the line toward Buffalo with arrival at Buffalo at 2:15 a.m. and Rochester at 6:15 a.m.

The NE and NY sections continue eastward. Hornell, N.Y., is the next icing station, with NE-98's scheduled arrival at 10:45 p.m. and NY-98 due at 12:45 a.m. From Hornell, NE-98 departs at 12:15 a.m., arriving in Susquehanna at 4:15 a.m., Port Jervis at 8 a.m., and Maybrook at 10 a.m. (connecting with the New Haven and handing off cars for Boston and other points northeast).

Meanwhile, NY-98 will leave Hornell at 2:45 a.m., Susquehanna at 7:15 a.m., and Port Jervis at 12:15 p.m., with an arrival at the Croxton, N.J., yard (across the Hudson from New York City) at

3:45 p.m. This timing allows cars to be switched, iced, and prepared for delivery to consignees or auction houses and unloading the following morning.

Cars are iced and then switched to car floats as requested by consignees. Tugboats move the floats across the river to piers, where cars are unloaded and the products distributed or put up for auction. Other cars may be diverted and sent to other locations by rail or float. Chapter 7 describes the ferry operations used to get cars to Manhattan.

Other Erie Chicago-New York trains also carried perishable traffic. For example, Erie's instructions called for Train 74 to carry all export fruit, juice grapes, and fruit bound for Newark. Trains 92 and 84 also carried New York Terminal perishables, often with cars that missed the cutoff times for 98 or cars that were diverted.

The instructions allowed Train 98 to carry nonperishable filler traffic, but this would be cut out and placed in a different train if necessary to make way for New York Terminal perishable traffic. In addition, NE-98 was restricted from carrying tank cars of flammable goods or open-top cars "containing lading which is liable to shift."

Although this description is particular to the Erie, the basic principles of coordinating connections with other railroads' perishable trains, prioritizing loads, blocking cars, and stopping only at major points to set out and pick up perishable cars, was followed by other railroads.

Sources: *Erie Railroad Company Instructions Covering Consist and Classification of Scheduled Freight Trains*, Office of Superintendent of Transportation, Cleveland (1950); "Handling Perishable Traffic," *Erie Railroad Magazine*, June 1944

12

Louisville & Nashville Train 18 arrives in Cincinnati in September 1965 from Atlanta with several express reefers carrying southeastern produce (two cars in ventilator service). *Louis A. Marre collection*

Returning and cleaning cars

Once refrigerator cars were unloaded, cars were returned to their home railroads or designated car shops. Refrigerator cars were not to be reloaded (as with other general-service freight cars) except by permission from their owners. Empties generally traveled in standard manifest trains unless they were urgently needed in a region, in which case they may warrant a special train movement.

Returning cars had to be deiced and cleaned. Owning railroads and car operators had multiple points equipped for doing this, usually at major yards or railroad shop facilities.

Cars were switched to clean-out tracks. Most work was done manually, requiring a worker to enter each bunker and chop, scoop, and throw out any remaining ice. Interiors were cleaned of residual waste, such as spilled or damaged products, torn or broken boxes or cases, and wood strips used to brace loads. Cars in top-ice service often had interior ice remaining.

Some railroads had tried using steam to clean cars, which worked well in bunkers but not bodies. In 1943, PFE started using hot water (190 degrees), sprayed down into the bunker or within the body. This worked well, and PFE estimated the process cut two-thirds off the time for cleaning a car.

Basic cleaning could take anywhere from 5 to 30 minutes per car depending upon the condition. The process was longer if a car's load had spoiled or become infested and required fumigation.

After cleaning, cars would be inspected for defects. Minor repairs were made on the spot or at a neighboring RIP (repair-in-place) track; major repairs may have required moving the car to another shop location. Cars would then be routed to the next harvest area as needed. Cars would generally receive a tag stapled to their placard board labeling them as clean and ready for loading.

Express reefer operations

As with standard freight parcels, shippers could pay a premium price for express shipment of refrigerated products. These shipments traveled in specially equipped cars (see chapter 2) in passenger or express trains, meaning a savings of 1 to 4 days of travel time (depending upon length of route) compared to standard perishable schedules. Along with other express and storage mail, this was known as head-end traffic, as it was carried at the head end of these trains, **12**.

In the days when most main routes hosted multiple passenger trains, head-end traffic was generally carried by secondary trains. For example, on the Northern Pacific, it was the *Mainstreeter*, not the premier *North Coast Limited*, that carried head-end cars (and often had more head-end cars than passenger cars). Most major railroads also operated unnamed trains that were entirely head-end traffic (some were known officially or unofficially as *Fast Mail* or *Mail and Express*).

Perishables that were the most sensitive to spoilage or damage and had the shortest shelf lives were most commonly shipped via express. Strawberries were the most common perishable express shipment,

Dozens of express refrigerator cars await loading at the Railway Express Agency terminal in Jacksonville, Fla., around 1940. *Railway Express Agency*

while others were cherries, grapes, nectarines, and plums. In addition, the first products of a season (oranges, grapefruit, peaches, and even some lettuce) were often shipped by express because they could attract higher prices on their first few days on the market. Other common refrigerated express included cut flowers, live plants, and fresh fish and other seafood.

Express reefers were operated by Railway Express Agency, with cars either owned by REA, owned by an individual railroad but leased by REA, or operated by the railroad under REA direction. (Operations were the same; what differed was bookkeeping in how mileage rates and fees were disbursed.)

Shippers would call REA for an express shipment. As railroads did with freight reefers, REA would try to gather cars at locations in preparation for particular harvests. A local freight or switch crew would drop off cars at a convenient siding near a growing area or at a packing shed or packing house.

Another option was a shipping terminal, such as REA's Jacksonville, Fla., facility, **13**. The largest in the country, it had a refrigerated storage area, covered platforms, and a large dock for incoming trucks, and it sent out many cars of refrigerated goods as well as standard express.

After being picked up and iced, express reefers were switched into passenger or express trains that operated on passenger schedules. If there were enough cars to warrant, a string of reefers could operate as a solid train—usually running as a second section of a scheduled express or passenger train, or sometimes as an extra. This simplified icing cars. An example was Illinois Central, which would operate solid trains of strawberries northbound out of Louisiana.

Icing express cars could be done at a conventional dock if a solid train was involved; otherwise, it was common to ice individual cars and small blocks of express reefers with portable ice trucks (see photo 20 on page 96).

At trains' originating terminals, passenger consists were placed along platforms first. Switch engines would add express reefers and other head-end cars to the consists as they became available (such as from connecting trains or inbound from pickup by locals), **14**.

En route, cars were switched in and out of consists as needed. A switch engine was often used, but the train's locomotive could also be used at smaller stations. At destination terminals, switchers would pull express cars after trains were spotted.

Express reefers were also often used to carry standard express shipments when not in refrigerated service. Express refrigerator service declined by the late 1950s, and by the 1960s, most express reefers still in service were used just for nonrefrigerated parcels.

Declining traffic

Perishable loads began declining after World War II and continued dropping steadily through the 1970s. By the 1950s and 60s, more food was being processed, with less fresh produce shipped long distances. Highways were improving and trucks were taking more traffic and delivering it sooner.

Out west, PFE carloadings peaked at 460,000 in 1946, dropped but held steady into the early 1950s, but after 1953 continued a steady decline: about 300,000 in 1960 and just over 200,000 in 1970. The trend was similar in other areas.

The ice-bunker reefer was becoming obsolete in the late 1960s as railroads transitioned to mechanical cars for produce as well as frozen goods. Most carriers pulled their ice docks by the early 1970s; the last, PFE, shut down the last of its icing platforms in September 1973. Some TIV (top-ice vegetable) shipping continued, either in ice cars or obsolete mechanical cars with equipment removed, with icing done by shippers.

Railroads and shippers began experimenting with piggyback for refrigerated shipments around 1960, hoping it would slow the loss of perishable traffic, **15**. FGE bought its first 50 trailers that year, and acquired 735 trailers by 1962. Pacific Fruit Express followed, buying 400 trailers and 200 flatcars in 1961, eventually owning 3,300 by 1968. Other operators included Santa Fe and New York Central.

With Pennsy and RF&P, Atlantic Coast Line and Seaboard Air Line both began running all-piggyback perishable reefer trains on a regular basis from southern Florida to New York City in 1961.

Piggyback didn't prove dependable enough or flexible enough for

A New Orleans Union Passenger Terminal switcher shoves four express reefers and two other head-end cars toward the terminal in 1954. *James G. LaVake*

perishable customers. Piggyback still wasn't as fast as trucks, and by the 1960s, demanding customers (now largely chain supermarkets with their own supply warehouses) wanted just-in-time delivery, coordinated for inventory control. Piggyback service didn't allow for rollers: shipments had to be directly consigned.

As carloads dropped, railroads were no longer able to run as many entire trains of perishables, instead handling cars in blocks in manifest trains. This caused schedules to slide, connections to be missed, and cars to be delayed—which led to more shippers opting for trucks.

The Penn Central merger and collapse led to massive car delays along many lines east of Chicago, including the critical New York market. Western roads were no longer able to guarantee times for shipments to those areas.

A last gasp for Southern Pacific was a service in the mid-1970s dubbed

the "Salad Bowl Express," with lettuce out of California bound for New York. Cars originated at Roseville and were handed off to UP at Ogden, to C&NW at North Platte, and then to Conrail at Chicago. In summer 1976, the service generated 225 cars a day and moved 9,000 loads in 1977. However, this dropped to 4,000 cars in 1978.

Pacific Fruit Express was disbanded in 1978, with cars divided between owners SP and UP. By 1979, just 10 percent of perishable traffic went by rail. No new mechanical refrigerator cars had been built since 1971, and many carriers were scrapping their fleets.

Modern operations

The number of mechanical reefers dropped dramatically, under 9,000 by 2000, with two main owners: Union Pacific and Burlington Northern Santa Fe. Most remaining refrigerator traffic

was in frozen foods, mainly frozen potatoes out of the Northwest, juice from Florida, and frozen foods from California. In 2001, BNSF reported its reefer business comprised 40 percent frozen vegetables (mainly potatoes), 33 percent frozen food (meat, fish, and poultry), and just 20 percent fresh produce.

Union Pacific in 2000 launched its Express Lane produce trains. This was a joint operation with CSX to bring western produce to eastern markets. The trains originate in two regions. One loads in California's San Joaquin Valley (carrots, celery, citrus, melons) and is classified at Fresno. The other comes from the Pacific Northwest (Idaho and Oregon potatoes and onions).

Cars from the two regions are consolidated and blocked at North Platte. Originally two trains were assembled: one bound for New York (providing 8-day service to New York

A Seaboard Air Line switcher backs toward a solid train of Fruit Growers Express piggyback trailers at the railroad's Richmond, Va., interchange with Richmond, Fredericksburg & Potomac in 1961. *J. Parker Lamb, Jr.*

Tropicana's Juice Train has been operating since 1970. Two CSX GE diesels pull the train northbound out of Bradenton, Fla., at Big Manatee River in 1999. *Scott A. Hartley*

Nonperishable reefer loading

Ice-bunker cars were sometimes used for dry lading. Here, Santa Fe cars are being loaded with storage mail during the Christmas rush. *Trains magazine collection*

The first priority of freight reefers (not including privately owned packing company cars and other brine-tank reefers) was seasonal fruit and vegetable traffic, and in peak seasons, these cars would be expedited back to various harvest areas for loading.

In off-peak times, these cars were used for dry, clean, nonperishable lading, especially goods that required protection from extreme hot or cold but didn't require refrigeration.

Canned goods and beverages were the primary lading, making up a third of total refrigerator-car loads (see the chart on page 67).

Another common lading was storage mail or less-than-carload (LCL) traffic. Railroads were still handling a lot of LCL through the 1950s, and reefers would often be used to carry parcels, express packages, or storage mail during busy periods, mainly the Christmas rush.

City and 9-day service to Boston) and the other to Waycross, Ga.

The service was successful, with 35,000 loads moved in 2001. Although railcars took twice the transit time of trucks, the service was half the cost. The railroad has continued to expand the service, actually increasing its reefer fleet in the 2000s with the addition of new 64- and 72-foot Trinity cars. BNSF acquired new Trinity cars as well.

In late 2017, the Union Pacific acquired Railex LLC, a company with cold storage outlets in Wallula, Wash., Delano, Calif., and Rotterdam, N.Y. The railroad had been carrying solid trains and blocks

of cars among the points for Railex, including frozen foods as well as fresh produce.

Arguably the best-known modern operation is the Juice Train, a series of unit trains and block shipments traveling from Tropicana's production plant in Bradenton, Fla., **16**. The original train debuted in 1970 with 150 100-ton refrigerator cars (built by FGE). Trains of 60 cars traveled 1,214 miles twice a week to a distribution center in South Kearny, N.J. (New York City area), making the trip in just over 43 hours.

The service was successful enough to grow to 5- and 6-day-a-week service, and Tropicana now has more

than 350 white, orange, and blue cars of several types, including reefers and insulated boxcars (to carry beverages not requiring refrigeration). The Kearny facility was replaced by one in Jersey City in 1991. Originally running on Seaboard Coast Line/RF&P/Penn Central, through mergers, the run is now all on CSX.

Another route was added in 1997: Bradenton-Cincinnati (1,063 miles), with two 30-or-so car trains a week, making the trip in 49 hours.

Recently, cars have begun traveling to southern California as well. Tropicana parent Pepsico actively solicits backhauls in the cars, which return by regular (non-unit) trains.

1

CHAPTER SIX

Making ice and icing reefers

Keeping bunker refrigerator cars cool required ice—and lots of it. Each car needed an initial load of at least five tons of ice, with an additional ton or two added each day to replace the ice that melted while the car was in transit.

A platform worker uses a pickaroon to slide a block of ice to his partner, who will chop it with his ice bar to fill the car's bunker. The action is at the Pacific Fruit Express platform on the Southern Pacific at Roseville, Calif., which could simultaneously handle trains of 50 and 78 cars on each side. *Jim Morley*

At the apex of the ice-bunker car era in the late 1940s, railroads and car owners annually used more than 13 million tons of ice to supply the 700 icing platforms in service across the country. The Santa Fe alone in 1951 required 516,693 tons of ice to service 243,160 cars at its 50-plus icing stations.

Initially, this meant cutting, or harvesting, natural ice from lakes and rivers, but later, most ice was manufactured. This ice was delivered to icing stations or platforms, where workers would swarm atop strings of cars, chopping large blocks of ice and dropping it into car bunkers, **1**.

Icing cars and coordinating the supply of ice with the operation of individual icing platforms and ice manufacturing plants kept thousands of workers employed through the 1960s. We'll look first at how ice was acquired and made, and then at the icing platforms and the icing process.

Natural ice

Through the 1800s, all ice used by railroads (as well as other consumers) was harvested—cut from lakes and ponds in the winter. Known as natural ice, it was cut into blocks by workers and stored in nearby ice sheds. These large buildings were designed to store enough ice each winter season to last through the following summer and fall.

Ice harvesting areas were sometimes located adjacent to a railroad icing station, but more often, the ice would have to be shipped to ice houses located at icing stations that didn't have a nearby natural source. Cold locations, especially with early subzero temperatures, were ideal for harvesting ice.

Some natural ice plants used existing calm lakes or ponds, but many had man-made ponds that were flooded or rivers that were dammed to create smooth, clear ice. With artificial ponds, the depth of the water could be controlled, which resulted in a smoother, more uniform product.

Harvesting ice was labor intensive. As ice began freezing, workers would plow or scrape off any snowfall that would slow the freezing process (or

2 Before power equipment was widely used, horse-drawn cutting plows made multiple passes across the ice to form deep parallel grooves. *Library of Congress*

3 Workers inserted heavy bars into the grooves, snapping off ice into small sheets that could easily be floated to shore. *Library of Congress*

cause uneven ice depth). Harvest time depended upon the region and weather, typically starting in January. Some extremely cold areas allowed multiple ice harvests each season.

Cutting began when the ice had reached the desired thickness (usually 14"–20"). A straight groove was made across the pond. Horse-drawn tools were used through the 1910s, making multiple passes with a "cutting plow"—a long saw blade—to make a cut several inches deep, **2**. Parallel grooves were then made by successive passes with the cutting plow using a guide placed in the neighboring groove to ensure uniform width. The desired size varied by railroad, and it was 22" for Pacific Fruit Express.

The process was repeated for perpendicular grooves to the specified size. Some made them square, others rectangular. Chicago & North Western instructions called for ice to be at least 14" thick and blocks not to exceed 24" x 48".

A crew then placed large bars as levers into the grooves to snap loose large panels that could be floated to the edge of the pond where ice was collected, **3**. The large panels were then broken into smaller sections and, finally, into individual blocks. The blocks were moved by conveyor to the ice house, where they were stacked tightly in storage rooms or loaded onto cars for transport to other ice houses, **4**.

Mechanical cutters replaced horse-drawn saws at most locations by the late 1910s, **5**. These featured large gas-powered saws that notched or cut the ice following grooves, with blocks divided and collected as before.

The weight of natural ice blocks varied with the thickness of the ice when it was harvested. Natural blocks were usually smaller than artificial ice blocks: about 175 to 275 pounds compared to 300 to 400 pounds for manufactured blocks.

Early ice houses were generally wood-framed, wood-sheathed structures with multiple interior storage rooms. Some were uninsulated, relying upon the mass of ice to maintain the cold (some loss was always expected). Some ice houses had insulated walls, generally

4 Men wrestle ice blocks into position with pickaroons and tongs, lining them up to be hoisted into the adjoining ice house (background). *Library of Congress*

5 Power equipment, including large gas-powered circular saws, sped the harvest process. This is a New York Central crew at Carthage, N.Y., in February 1947. *New York Central*

double walls packed with sawdust.

The largest could hold upwards of 40,000 tons or more of ice. Although some 19th century ice houses spread sawdust atop stacks of ice as insulation, the practice wasn't widespread, as the sawdust (or any other material) made it difficult to slide and move the blocks, and could contaminate ice bunkers and plug cars' drain outlets.

Natural ice continued to be a significant source into the 1930s, but issues with polluted water, inconsistent block size, and the need to ship it large distances made it less practical as mechanical plants became more

efficient. The last natural ice harvests occurred in the early 1950s.

Mechanical ice plants

By the 1920s, mechanical refrigeration technology had advanced enough to make it practical to manufacture large ice blocks, **6**. These plants were sometimes owned by railroads or car owners, including Santa Fe, PFE, and Fruit Growers Express. Many plants were privately owned, with railroads and car owners contracting for the ice.

Railroad-owned mechanical plants were often located adjacent to an icing platform, but they would also supply

6

Ice is stacked in layers in the storage room at the Erie Railroad's ice plant at Marion, Ohio. The manufactured ice blocks are uniform in size. *Erie Railroad*

7

Ice blocks are being moved from a New York Central ice plant into older boxcars and refrigerator cars in the early 1900s. *New York Central*

ice to other locations. These modern plants featured up-to-date construction with concrete walls, improved insulation materials, and refrigerated storage rooms that kept stored ice blocks intact.

The process used a large tank (or multiple tanks) of calcium chloride brine, supercooled down to near zero degrees by the ammonia process (the salt in the water kept it from freezing). These tanks were about 5 feet deep and had circulating pumps to ensure consistent temperature throughout.

A series of tall stainless steel containers (called cans) were filled with water and lowered, using a hoist, into the brine. The brine tank was covered by a series of hatches that were opened for cans to be lowered, and when closed allowed workers to walk on top. Depending on the installation, this was done in groups of two to six cans at a time. They would freeze in about 24 hours.

The Great Northern plant at Hillyard, Wash., for example, had two 20 x 40-foot brine tanks. Cans were filled and pulled two at a time, with a pair of cans pulled out of each tank every 20 minutes for a 12-block-per-hour (4,800-pound) capacity, just over 57 tons per day (21,000 tons per year). Manufactured ice blocks weighed 300 to 400 pounds (PFE's 300-pounders measured 10" x 21" x 42").

Newer plants had much greater capacity. Modernized in 1954, PFE's Ogden plant could hold 6,400 cans in four separate brine tanks and produce 4,750 blocks (700 tons) daily, using an automated process with only one worker running a hoist. The largest plants had impressive storage capacities: PFE's Roseville, Calif., facility could store 53,000 tons of ice on site.

Along with their own plants, railroads contracted with local ice dealers. This was sometimes done just for peak periods, although sometimes year-round. Contractors also often iced individual cars (or small blocks of cars) and provided emergency icing services. Railroads would also trade ice if needed (even rivals PFE and ATSF would do this to save the expense of shipping ice longer distances).

Moving ice

Whether natural or manufactured, ice blocks often had to be moved from manufacturing plants and storage sheds to icing stations that lacked manufacturing facilities. Blocks could be carried in standard boxcars—doing this in the winter was ideal, resulting in the least amount of melting, **7**.

By the 1920s and later, this was often the duty of old or obsolete refrigerator cars that had been converted to ice service, **8**. These usually had bunkers removed to provide more interior room, and offered insulation, resulting in less melting than boxcars. Railroads usually repainted and relettered cars in ice service, and they could have considerable fleets devoted to it (more than 300 on PFE at one time).

Typical cars would carry 20–25 tons of ice (PFE figured 164 blocks per car). This could mean a remote icing station might receive dozens of cars a day to supply ice.

At ice plants, blocks would be conveyed along platforms that were at car-floor height and slid into cars, where they would be stacked. Workers in storage rooms and inside cars wore crimp-on spikes to give them sure footing, and they used self-closing tongs to pull blocks into position.

Delivering ice also required a platform at door level, allowing the blocks to be slid from the cars onto conveyors that elevated them to the ice house, **9**.

As you can imagine, moving 300-plus-pound blocks of ice was not only challenging but dangerous. Blocks could slide unpredictably (as could feet). Ice in storage would sometimes fuse together (especially on lower layers of stacks, or in nonrefrigerated sheds) and have to be chipped and pried apart—preferably without shattering the blocks. Blocks in storage for long periods could also develop rough edges of snow (think freezer burn), making them difficult to slide and maneuver.

Obviously, by the time many ice blocks were used, they weren't perfectly dimensioned. They might be chipped, cracked, or oddly shaped, but as long as they still fit on the conveyor chains, they would be used.

This wood American Refrigerator Transit car with archbar trucks, built in 1911, was assigned to company ice service by the time of this 1939 photo. *J. Harold Geissel*

Workers unload ice cars at PFE's Hinkle, Ore., facility (left). A few blocks are on the conveyor heading upward. The icing platform is at right. *Union Pacific*

This New York Central island-style platform has both upper and lower levels. The boxes along the deck store salt. The ice plant is at right and has an overhead conveyor for moving ice to the dock. *New York Central*

The upper deck was used to provide crushed ice to brine-tank (meat) refrigerator cars. This is the Erie platform at Marion, Ohio, which served trains having both meat and produce cars. *Erie Railroad*

The Minneapolis & St. Louis maintained a small icehouse and platform at its Peoria, Ill., terminal, shown here in 1949. *Bill Armstrong*

Icing stations

Railroads and refrigerator car lines operated hundreds of icing stations across the country. The largest number were operated by Santa Fe (53 regular stations in the 1940s) and Pacific Fruit Express (51 stations in 1952, served by 18 ice plants), **1**. These numbers didn't include emergency stations. Since cars required re-icing approximately every 24 hours, locations tended to be spaced 250–400 miles apart on main routes and were often located at major yards, division points, and terminals.

The specific design of icing platforms varied by owner and period, but all followed similar principles. (Generally an icing station referred to a location providing icing service, including the dock and all supporting structures and equipment, while the structure itself was called a platform, deck, or dock.)

Most were wood framed, with a deck at car-roof level (about 14 feet), and they were adjacent to an icehouse. A platform could serve a single track on one side or be an island-style design with a track on either side. On these, a conveyor passed above one of the tracks to bring ice from the icehouse to the platform, although some newer facilities had underground tunnels to convey ice, **10**.

A covered roof or shelter above the deck was an option for sheltering workers and preventing excessive ice melt. Lights were placed along the platform for night operations.

Some platforms had an additional working deck above the main deck. This was used for delivering crushed ice and salt for meat reefers with brine tanks, with the main deck used for conventional RS (produce) reefers, **11**.

Many decks had flush edges, so workers simply stepped directly from the icing platform to the car. Some platforms had small hinged aprons that folded down from the platform to the car roofs. A narrow ramp was attached to the edge of the platform and dropped to the car's running board. This was used to slide ice from the platform to the car's hatches. This would be moved as a crew worked its way from car to car.

Platform length and total car capacity varied greatly: Most were the equivalent of at least 5 car-lengths. The largest could serve 50 cars or more (some island-type platforms could serve 100 or more cars). The longer the platform, the more cars that could be iced at once, thus the faster the service.

Stations along main routes that served solid trains of perishable traffic had the longest platforms. These major stations had multiple platforms and tracks. A remodeling of PFE's Laramie, Wyo., station on the Union Pacific in 1947 meant that 248 cars could be serviced at once. This was the result of a new island platform with 85 spots on each side, plus the older dock which could handle 78 cars.

There were plenty of smaller docks in service as well, located on lines that didn't see solid trains of refrigerator cars, **12**. They were commonly located at yards in division points or junction points.

At early docks (and small docks that serviced only a few cars), ice was moved manually. Most platforms used a conveyor, typically a chain with lugs, that traveled in a recessed slot along the deck to carry blocks of ice from the adjacent ice house.

The ice house could be adjacent to the dock or be separate but connected by an overhead conveyor. The PFE dock on the UP at Kansas City, for

Judging by the large stockpile of ice and the many bags of salt, these workers are performing initial icing on these Santa Fe reefers at Illinois Central's platform at Stuyvesant Docks in New Orleans. *Illinois Central*

example, ran down the center of the yard with a track on either side and had an overhead conveyor at one end.

Platforms required a supply of salt, which could be stored in barrels, bags, or large boxes built into the platform, **13**. Large docks could use 5 tons or more per day in hot weather. These would have a bulk salt storage house, usually at ground level at one end of the platform, **14**. A vertical bucket-style conveyor carried salt to the platform, where it was moved in carts.

An icing station would also have a storage area for the portable charcoal or alcohol heaters used to keep cars from freezing in cold weather (see the sidebar on page 94).

Tracks at icing platforms were almost always double-ended, whether on main lines or in yards, to make it easier for trains to be iced without delay. Another track or two (through or stub-ended) would be next to the ice house for delivering ice (along with a platform and conveyor), salt (in bags, barrels, or bulk in boxcars), and boxcars of heaters being delivered or returned.

Inside the ice house, workers would

The small building holds bulk salt, which is conveyed to the top deck. The conveyor dumps salt into the cart, which travels the platform to replenish the salt boxes on the car-height deck. *New York Central*

slide blocks of ice onto the conveyor chain that led to the dock; the chain on the dock would then carry the ice along the dock to the car locations. The goal was to have the ice in place when the train arrived.

By the 1940s, large docks had PA systems for communication between the dock and icehouse.

Platform operations

Chapter 5 explains train operations and the various protective services available, which covers when cars will be iced. Shippers could choose several options, which varied by the lading being carried, distance being covered, and prevailing weather and outdoor temperatures.

Workers ice a string of Western Fruit Express cars loaded with apples at Great Northern's Appleyard in Wenatchee, Wash., in the early 1940s. *Great Northern*

The Burlington's ice dock at Denver in 1949 had carts to haul salt and crushed ice along the deck, with a rolling chute to direct salt into hatch openings. The conveyor chain carried ice blocks when needed. *Earl Cochran*

The icing station would have advance notice of each train arriving, including a summary of each car's icing requirements (listed on a car's waybill and summarized on train lists). This was originally done by telegraph, and by the 1930s, by teletype and then telephone.

Pneumatic tubes were used at some stations to send messages, train lists, waybill information, and other paperwork between office, icehouse, and platform. All of this ensured that, by the time a train arrived, the icing station knew exactly what it was getting.

Inbound traffic could mean a solid train of 50 to 100 refrigerator cars, a manifest freight with a 10-car block of reefers (one reason reefers were commonly blocked together at the front of trains was to enable the entire block to be at the platform at once), or a train with two or three refrigerator cars.

On the deck, one or more workers would pull blocks coming from the storage room and redirect them to the platform chain, where other workers would pull blocks off at the approximate car locations.

Once trains were stopped or individual cars spotted, the train or cars had to be "blue flagged"—blue tags attached to both ends of the train indicating that workers were present on the cars. Some platforms had small permanent signals with blue semaphores to do this. The train was not allowed to move until blue flags were removed.

If the train was long and the dock was short, the train would have to move and repeat the process, making for a much longer station stop. This is why railroads on major perishable routes tried to match train length to ice platform capacity on each route.

When the train was in position, an inspector or inspectors with lists of car requirements walked the train and opened all of the hatches of cars requiring ice (leaving hatches closed on cars not needing ice). A worker checked each bunker and estimated the amount of ice required in each, chalking this on the hatch and noting on cards or paperwork to maintain a record of each car by number and ice amount.

Some trains might have all cars requiring the same treatment, but it was much more common for a hotshot perishable train to have a mix of cars. Even if most required standard re-icing with coarse ice, there were probably a few with interior top ice that required no bunker ice, some where the shipper requested initial ice only with no re-icing, and some in ventilator service (which may have to have hatches opened or closed depending upon the temperature). There could also be a few meat reefers requiring a mix of crushed ice and salt, and perhaps a car or two of frozen goods that required ice and heavy salt.

Icing cars

Although ice blocks weigh up to 400 pounds, they aren't put into the car that way. A solid block dropped into a bunker would damage the grates at the bottom of the bunker, and large blocks won't settle properly in the bunkers, leaving too much air space.

Instead, the ice is chopped into smaller pieces as it's added to the car. Any given car may have instructions to use one of three types of ice: chunk, coarse, or crushed. Chunk is the largest, with pieces weighing up to 75 pounds (a quarter of a full block). The most

A hoist attached to a boom on the icing machine lowers an alcohol heater into the bunker of a Santa Fe car at Argentine, Kan., in the 1950s. *Santa Fe*

common is coarse, with pieces ranging from 10 to 20 pounds each. Crushed is the smallest (baseball- or softball-sized pieces) and is used in meat cars equipped with brine tanks instead of standard ice bunkers.

How many workers and crews were on duty depended upon the railroad or owner, along with the capacity of the dock and the train schedules and speeds. A terminal dock that pre-iced cars for delivery to local packing houses would have fewer crews, as speed wasn't as important as a mainline dock that re-iced hotshot trains on tight schedules.

The basic tools of a dock worker were the pickaroon, or pike, a long pole with a pair of sharp, triangular points at angles. This was used for maneuvering and positioning blocks. Another pole with a heavy U-shaped prong at the end—an ice bar—was used for chopping the ice blocks. Both were kept sharp.

Each bunker was worked by a two-man crew. They would drop the platform apron to the car as

The mechanical icing machine on the PFE dock at Laramie, Wyo., rides on rails atop the platform. The operator selects the ice size and can direct ice into either hatch opening. *Union Pacific*

close to the hatches as possible. One worker started by chopping the ice already in the bunker, getting it to settle downward and removing any air pockets. His partner would use a pickaroon to tip the ice off the chain (this—"spotting your ice"—could be done before cars are in position).

The man on the platform would slide a block across the ramp to his partner on the car, who would take the ice and chop it to the proper sizes with his bar while feeding it into the bunker hatch, **15**. Meanwhile, his partner on the dock was maneuvering another block to the ramp. The process

Heaters

Small heaters were used to keep loads from freezing in cold weather. Early heaters were charcoal. They were loaded with fuel, lit, and would burn until extinguished or the fuel ran out. Later charcoal heaters could have the fuel burn rate adjusted for more control.

By the 1940s, heaters like the pictured model from Preco were alcohol fueled. They had pilot lights and thermostatic control, which allowed the desired temperature to be set. These didn't have to be removed based on outdoor temp, as did charcoal heaters, since they would simply shut themselves off if the temperature rose.

Here's a guideline showing outdoor temperatures (degrees F) at which heaters in refrigerator cars were lighted for various commodities.

Commodity	Light heater or heaters when outside temperature drops to the following:		Extinguish heaters when outside temperature rises above:	
	First Heater	Second Heater	First Heater	Second Heater
Sweet potatoes	25°	5°	25°	10°
Potatoes	20°	-5°	20°	-5°
Mixed potatoes & onions	20°	-5°	20°	-5°
Tomatoes	20°	5°	20°	10°
Apples, avocados, pears	10°	-5°	10°	-5°
Cranberries, onions	10°	-5°	10°	-5°
Citrus fruit (not limes)	5°	-5°	5°	-5°
Limes	20°	-5°	20°	-5°
Celery	-10°	—	-10°	—
Perishables not specified	15°	-5°	15°	-5°
Butter	25°	5°	25°	10°
Beverages (not beer)	25°	5°	25°	10°
Beer	20°	5°	20°	10°
Canned goods	5°	-5°	5°	-5°

Source: *Service Instructions for Perishable Freight*, Western Pacific (1949)

continued, alternating between the near and far hatches, until the bunker was full, and then the men would move to the next bunker. They may have to put the hatch plug and cover in place and latch it, or this might be done by a separate worker.

If salt was required, it would be added above the ice load. How it was supplied varied. Some kept salt in boxes atop the platform, to be shoveled in as needed. Some used large wheelbarrow-style carts with chutes aimed into hatches, **16**. Others used 100-pound

sacks, making it easy to determine how much was being added (as waybills specified a percentage of salt to ice), **13**. Thus if a waybill specified 10 percent ice and workers added four 300-pound blocks (1,200 pounds) to a bunker, they knew to add 120 pounds of salt.

An efficient crew could re-ice a car in about 2 minutes, with 3–5 blocks required per bunker. Initial icing at terminals took longer, as each empty bunker would require 16–18 blocks of ice to be chopped into place. Overall speed in re-icing a train depended

upon how many cars each crew was responsible for. For hot trains, more crew members would be on duty. For manual icing, railroads usually figured total icing time to take about 1½–2 minutes per car.

When all hatches were closed and all workers accounted for, the blue flags would be removed and the train could continue (or for cuts of cars, a switcher could couple to the cars and move them).

If icing was done at a division point requiring an engine change or cars to be switched, this could occur during icing. In these cases, the engine or other cars would cut off before the cars were blue-flagged.

Cars and loads may be inspected at icing stations as well. A side door may be opened to take a car's temperature reading or produce sample. Bananas, for example, had samples pulled and checked for internal temp by a probe thermometer. Mechanical cars would be checked for fuel, operation, and temperature.

Depending upon the protective services required, workers may have had to reset hatches for ventilation or add or remove heaters. If heaters were required, they would be loaded with charcoal, lighted, lowered by their hooks into bunkers—usually one in each bunker. When they were added, warning placards were placed on the hatches and side doors to alert workers of the presence of carbon monoxide.

Alcohol-fueled heaters came along in the 1940s. These were more efficient, had pilot lights, and could be thermostatically controlled and set at desired temperatures.

Heaters could be added and removed manually using a hook or pickaroon (often with charcoal heaters, photo 4 on page 68). The heavier alcohol heaters were often moved by a small hoist, **17**.

At terminal or interchange locations, heaters might have to be removed. For the most part, heaters stayed on their home railroads. Once pulled out of the bunkers and extinguished, they were stored. Any foreign-road heaters were shipped by LCL (less-than-carload) service back to their home lines.

This unique PFE machine at Eugene, Ore., built by Preco in 1958, is self-propelled and carries its ice supply on a trailer behind the unit. *Union Pacific*

An example of ice platform operations at a terminal location is provided by the UP at Kansas City, where eastbound UP perishable trains and blocks arrive and will be interchanged with other railroads.

An inbound train pulls to the icing platform, and the road locomotives cut off. A switcher pulls off all nonperishable cars from the rear and takes them to the dead-freight yard. As soon as the switcher is clear, the cars are blue-flagged and the reefers are iced.

When the icing is complete, blue flags come down and a switcher pulls the reefers from either end, taking them to the adjacent perishable yard for sorting. They will then be delivered in blocks to connecting railroads, all of which have specific cutoff times for their priority freight trains.

Icing, as a protective service, was billed to car owners. For example, PFE provided protective services on SP and UP lines, so if a PFE car was iced off-line—let's say on the Erie—then PFE would be billed by the Erie for that service.

Icing machines

As labor costs rose following World War II, railroads looked for mechanical solutions that would both cut costs and speed icing times. The result was the mechanical icing machine, first used by the Santa Fe at Bakersfield, Calif., in 1949 and followed by PFE in 1951 at Fresno. Many additional installations followed across the country—PFE eventually had machines at 10 icing platforms.

The two main builders were Link-Belt and Preco. Features differed, but they operated on the same concept. The machine could be adapted to an existing dock, riding on a pair of parallel rails atop the car-height deck, **18**. On a few new installations, the machine rode on a railroad track, **19**.

Blocks of ice, fed by a conveyor chain (either running down the middle of the dock or on a conveyor above the ground-level track), are scooped into the machine, crushed, and fed into car bunkers by chutes overhanging the track. The operator, riding on the machine, can adjust the size of ice based on the requirements of each car. Large-capacity docks may have two or three machines working at once.

Power came from overhead electric wires. The machines used a trolley-like mechanism that slid along the wires as the machine moved.

A press release for Union Pacific's then-new $4 million icing platform at Kansas City in 1954 gave an example of a train of 71 reefers that was spotted at the platform at 4:15 a.m. and released 55 minutes later, at 5:10— about 50 seconds per car.

Some docks used another rail-mounted machine to deliver salt, which followed the icing machine down the dock.

One or two "follow-up" men would follow the machine, chopping any stray

20
A local ice contractor with a hoist truck tops off the bunkers of Santa Fe and ART reefers parked on a spur in Ohio in 1964. *J. David Ingles collection*

21
Top-ice machines (or "snow machines" or "slingers") blew finely crushed ice atop loads. The entire space above the load would be filled before the car was sealed. *Russell Lee, Library of Congress*

ice as needed and closing and securing the latches.

Portable icing

Icing of individual cars (or small groups of cars) wasn't always done at icing platforms. Instead, various lift trucks or hoists accomplished the task. This could be done either by a railroad service vehicle or by a local ice dealer or contractor, **20**.

This was commonly done with express reefers, both upon initial loading at remote field locations or at passenger station platforms, when only one or several cars on a train required re-icing.

Portable icing was also often done for single-car shipments, for cars that had been set out for repairs while loaded, or those on secondary or branch lines or other territory where there were no available icing platforms.

The car would be on a spur or team track where a truck could get access.

The service was usually provided by a contractor (often a local ice dealer). Ice blocks would be raised by an elevated truck bed, hoist, or conveyor and then chopped and dropped into bunkers as needed.

Top-icing

Top-icing is the process of blowing a layer of finely crushed ice over the entire load in a car, **21**. It was commonly done for leafy vegetables, carrots, and other produce to both control temperature and keep the humidity high. It was known as top-ice vegetable (TIV) service. Top-icing was done after initial loading of the car and could be reapplied en route if needed.

By the mid 1930s, many icing stations had top-icing machines, with 200 in service in the United States by 1941. Machines could be portable, mounted on a vehicle or trailer, or mounted on rails on an icing station deck.

For example, a rebuilding project in 1947 at the PFE icing station at Laramie, Wyo., included installation of eight new ice "slingers" that replaced older units dating to the late 1930s. They were located on rails on a lower platform at car-floor height and rolled to cars.

Chunk ice was fed to the machine, which crushed the ice and used an internal fan to blow it out of a flexible hose into the car. A worker in the car's open doorway moved the hose to spray the ice evenly across the load. The platform's earlier machines had been on the upper deck, requiring some maneuvering to get the hose down to top-ice the cars.

Older machines required 7–10 minutes per car; modern units, per a Santa Fe news release in 1960, took about 3 minutes per car.

After most icing stations were closed in 1973, many former ice cars (with bunkers removed) remained in

TIV service through the 1970s, with top ice applied by the shipper upon loading. Some older mechanical cars with refrigeration equipment removed were also converted to this service.

Precooling plants

Precooling plants were located in many harvest areas. The first was PFE's, which began service at Roseville in 1909. Cars were switched to the plant from loading, with loads retaining field heat (70 degrees or above). To remove the heat, flexible canvas ducts were connected to the doors and hatches. Cold air was blown into the doors and out the hatches. It took about 2 hours to get the load temperature down to 40 degrees, whereupon the car was switched out, iced, and ready to move.

Santa Fe's San Bernardino precooling plant, located adjacent to the icing station, opened in 1910 with an initial capacity of 32 cars (16 on each side of the dock), **22**.

By the 1940s, the process had evolved and improved, with 20-degree air being blown through the car at a high rate for 20 minutes and then the airflow direction was reversed. A car could be precooled in under an hour, which was much faster than the 24 hours or more it took to precool a load in a cold-storage room.

There were also portable precooling units mounted on trucks, **23**. These pumped refrigerated air into cars and could service cars in any area from a remote field to a packing shed track. As chapter 4 explains, lettuce and other produce was sometimes vacuum precooled.

Demise

Railroads continued adding to and upgrading icing stations into the early 1960s, when it became apparent that the days of ice-bunker cars were limited. Many smaller icing stations closed as traffic levels dropped, and mechanical and insulated cars increased in numbers.

Santa Fe discontinued icing in 1971, and the Interstate Commerce Commission gave PFE permission to close all its platforms in September 1973, ending the era of ice-bunker cars.

Santa Fe's precooling plant at San Bernardino, Calif., used flexible ductwork in hatches and doorways to push cold air at high volume and rapidly cooled loads.
Jack Delano, Library of Congress

A truck-mounted precooling unit cools a freshly loaded car of potatoes in Rio Grande County, Colo., in October 1939. Note the ductwork in the car door behind the truck.
Arthur Rothstein, Library of Congress

1

CHAPTER SEVEN

Produce terminals and final customers

The Chicago & North Western's Chicago "potato yard" covered 60 acres and could receive more than 500 refrigerator cars for its daily auctions and sales. It served more than 20,000 cars each year. Cars from nine owners or lessees can be seen in this 1957 view. *Chicago & North Western*

Where do all those fruits and vegetables go? Many are shipped to individual customers such as food wholesalers, supermarket chains, and food processing companies. Through the 1940s and 1950s, tens of thousands of cars went to large terminals where produce was auctioned or sold directly, **1**.

2

Two Pacific Fruit Express reefers and one from American Refrigerator Transit await unloading at a Roanoke, Va., produce wholesaler around 1950. *Trains magazine collection*

Private buyers

As with other freight, a shipper might sell a carload of fruits or vegetables directly to a buyer. This could mean a wholesaler in a large or small city, a canning or processing company, a supermarket chain (or food-buying co-op of independent store owners), or a hotel or restaurant chain, **2–5**.

Most canneries and food-processing companies were located near harvest areas to minimize transportation costs. This was true for most canned and frozen vegetable and juice (including frozen concentrate) producers. Railroads often carried finished products from these factories, but most inbound produce was a short haul handled by trucks.

An exception was large-scale food processors that made a variety of products. One example was baby-food company Gerber, **6**. Gerber's products used a variety of fruits and vegetables, not all of which were available locally. Their factory, located in Fremont, Mich.,

received inbound shipments of produce by rail—photo **6** shows a steam switcher moving a cut of three ice-bunker cars into position.

Another example was food giant Campbell's, maker of soup and many other canned food products. Huge companies like Campbell's would often sign contracts in advance for products and then fill additional needs as necessary through wholesalers and brokers.

Campbell's did this with tomatoes through the 1940s, contracting with growers in the Lancaster, Pa., area to have carloads shipped via the Pennsylvania Railroad to Campbell's factory in Camden, N.J. The factory canned all of its tomato soup (its most popular product) for the year in the July-to-September harvest season, up to 10 million cans per day. To serve this, the Pennsy delivered blocks of cars daily, 30–40 cars at a time. Campbell's also received inbound vegetables by truck and ship.

Independent buyers might receive refrigerator cars at their own docks or use team tracks at local railroad yards, stations, or sidings and off-load products directly into trucks, **7**.

Produce terminals

Large produce terminals were located in almost every major city: Chicago, New York, Philadelphia, Boston, Baltimore, Atlanta, Pittsburgh, Cleveland, Indianapolis, and others. Many of these terminals and markets still exist, albeit now served by trucks instead of rail.

Into the 1960s, however, railroads were the primary method of serving these markets. Local suppliers might also bring in products by truck, and terminals in coastal areas also often offered imported produce as well, taken directly from ships. The exact logistics, size, and scope of operations varied among individual markets and terminals, but the basic operations and functions were similar at each.

3 Fruit Growers Express no. 4011 is delivering a load to a Kansas City wholesaler around 1950. The 50-foot car is equipped with overhead ice bunkers, a rarity for U.S. lines. *C. Winters collection, Big Four Graphics*

4 This Soo Line leased car is in assigned service to a food company (stenciling in black box at left). It has a HEATER CAR placard on the door to warn workers of gases from heaters placed in bunkers. *J. David Ingles collection*

5 A PFE reefer is tucked behind a Chicago food wholesaler on the Chicago & North Western in the 1950s. City street trackage and tight spaces have great modeling potential. *Chicago & North Western*

Fruits and vegetables were a commodity—buyers could purchase produce from any number of sellers, and prices constantly fluctuated based on demand, supply, and perceived scarcity as well as a specific product's size, condition, and grade. If a heavy frost was predicted in Florida, citrus prices rose; if tomato growers had a record harvest, tomato prices would fall.

Most markets had auctions as part of their services, 8. Other products would be sold outright, much of this going through commission agents, 9. Commission agents would work with multiple distant sellers, negotiating with various buyers and selling shippers' products for a percentage of sales.

The chart on citrus markets in the 1940s (page 101) provides a glimpse of where carloads of produce headed after packing. Even though the final destination of most was retail sale, they took several routes to get there.

Buyers at markets included wholesalers and jobbers, 10. The largest of these would buy produce in large lots, taking them by truck to their own warehouses and selling them—via wagon and truck—to smaller buyers, including restaurants, hotels, individual grocery stores, and other customers, 11.

Many small jobbers were one-man operations. A jobber would buy enough produce to fill his truck or wagon, head out on his route to sell to customers, and then repeat the process each day, 12.

Individual stores, restaurants, and shop owners (including produce-cart owners) could also buy products at terminals. An advantage to this was getting the lowest possible prices, and the key disadvantage was time—most small business owners had to stay at their shops and restaurants, making it easier for them to deal with jobbers and wholesalers, even if the price was higher.

As chain stores grew in number through the 1940s and '50s, they began buying produce in large lots and taking them to their own warehouses for distribution. Chains would also sometimes buy directly from producers or through brokers, and take delivery of railcars directly.

A Pere Marquette steam locomotive switches three ice-bunker refrigerator cars at the Gerber baby food factory in Fremont, Mich., in the 1940s. *Gerber*

Brokers acted as intermediaries between buyers and sellers, matching needs and wants of each. Brokers could operate on a local, regional, or even national level.

Let's say a broker working with the A&P supermarket chain knew the company was looking for three carloads of oranges for its Cincinnati region warehouse. The broker would check market prices and locate, perhaps, a packing house in California that had earlier sent three rollers (unconsigned carloads that had been shipped without buyers). The cars were heading toward Chicago in Pacific Fruit Express cars on the Union Pacific, currently approaching Omaha, Neb.

The broker would negotiate a price between the shipper and A&P, and when the deal was done, the shipper would issue a revised waybill and routing. Upon receiving this, the UP would divert the cars in Omaha, and they would be switched out to their new route: Omaha to St. Louis on the Wabash, and then to Cincinnati on the Baltimore & Ohio.

Orange market in 1943-44

Methods of selling and distributing refrigerator carloads of Florida and California oranges in the 1943-44 season

Methods of distribution	Florida	California
	(by percentage)	
Terminal auctions	11	12
Terminal wholesalers & jobbers	38	55
Chain stores & co-op buying groups	33	28
Local buyers	5	—
Brokers	5	6

Final destinations		
Retail sale	72	81
Processors (juice and other)	24	11
Government programs	4	8

Terminal rail operations

At most markets, produce cars would arrive in the evening or overnight, so they would be unloaded and the products displayed first thing in the

Team tracks could be used for unloading produce, such as these 100-pound sacks of potatoes, directly into trucks. *Chicago & North Western*

Large produce markets usually featured auctions. Produce was put on display overnight, with auctions taking place first thing in the morning. This one is in New York City. *Arthur Rothstein, Library of Congress*

Commission agents worked on behalf of multiple sellers to negotiate sales to customers. This is in New York at Pennsylvania Railroad's Pier 29 in 1939. *Arthur Rothstein, Library of Congress*

morning. Buyers would begin arriving early. Auctions were conducted early, so the produce would be unloaded and sold quickly, **13**.

Some terminals had extensive indoor display areas, so cars were unloaded and the produce placed on display. At others, samples from each car would be placed, but full car unloading was up to the buyer. Carloads of produce coming in could either be sold outright or auctioned.

Most terminals handled all types of fruits and vegetables, but some specialized in specific products. Chicago's "potato yard" and Erie's New York Monmouth Street yard (grapes) were examples.

The Pittsburgh Produce Terminal served by the Pennsylvania, was an example of a large multiple-commodity yard, **14**. More than a dozen tracks, many with covered platforms between them, had a capacity of more than 400 cars (some yard space was shared with an adjoining less-than-carload terminal).

The facility had a large indoor terminal building (1,524 x 116 feet) for displaying and selling goods. Floor space was divided among consignees who auctioned shipments and those selling privately. Consignees received reports on cars in transit and then upon arrival; car diversions could happen up until the last minute.

As cars arrived and were switched into the yard, a card for each car was delivered to the produce office along with waybills. Samples were taken from the cars and put on display.

At Pittsburgh, about 20 percent of arriving cars were sold and reconsigned without being unloaded. These would be switched out and sent on their way that evening, often after being re-iced or top-iced by a truck in the yard. Technically, this was done by Fruit Growers Express, which provided protective services on Pennsylvania lines, but at Pittsburgh (and many other locations), FGE contracted with a local ice dealer to provide the services.

Among the most famous specialty yards was Chicago & North Western's Chicago potato yard, also known as the Wood Street Terminal, at the railroad's

New York's Washington Street Market, at Pier 29, is busy as wholesalers and other buyers load their trucks and wagons in 1939.

Arthur Rothstein, Library of Congress

Erie's Monmouth Yard

The chart highlights the carloads of grapes handled each year at Erie's Monmouth, N. J., yard. It lists the total number of carloads handled each year, followed by the number actually unloaded at Monmouth, the number unloaded at nearby Pavonia Yard, and the number of cars resold and diverted to other locations.

Grape loads																	
	1935	1936	1937	1938	1939	1940	1941	1942	1943	1944	1945	1946	1947	1948	1949	1950	1951
Monmouth	802	320	491	323	305	158	251	528	59	439	163	219	333	213	171	164	176
Pavonia	685	389	595	538	736	811	798	863	224	434	647	708	856	868	615	517	713
Diversions	2,596	2,039	2,712	2,124	2,566	2,540	2,267	1,964	241	1,184	762	1,446	1,455	1,601	1,124	1,177	916
Total cars	4,083	2,748	3,798	2,985	3,607	3,509	3,316	3,355	524	2,057	1,572	2,373	2,644	2,682	1,910	1,858	1,805

Source: *Erie Railroad Company Instructions Covering Consist and Classification of Scheduled Freight Trains,* Office of Superintendent of Transportation, Cleveland (1950)

The final destination for most fresh fruits and vegetables that began their journey by rail was retail sale, as at this A&P in Montgomery, Ala., in 1943. *John Vachon, Library of Congress*

Many small jobbers were one-man operations that bought enough produce at market each morning to fill a truck and then headed out directly to customers during the day. *Library of Congress*

Wood Street Yard. As the name implies, it specialized in potatoes but also handled onions and cabbage, **1**.

Wood Street was a 60-acre team-track facility that could handle 550 40-foot refrigerator cars at once, and it served more than 20,000 cars annually. Twenty stub-end tracks in ladder style were arranged in pairs, surrounded by a concrete apron. A 50-foot spacing between track pairs allowed room for trucks and other vehicles to maneuver and unload directly from cars.

The yard had lights for night operations, scales for weighing trucks, some tracks with covered platforms, and an adjoining office building for conducting business. Brokers, sellers, and agents largely worked in the yard itself, with trucks loading sold products directly from cars. As with the Pittsburgh terminal, cars that were diverted and resold would be iced by a truck in the yard and switched to outbound trains in the evening, **15**. The yard operated through the 1960s, but traffic dropped dramatically by the 1970s.

An example of a small-scale seasonal specialty yard was Erie's Monmouth Street Yard in Jersey City. The railroad dedicated several tracks in the yard to refrigerator cars during grape season, which ran from September through November.

The yard handled from 1,500 to 4,000 reefers of juice grapes each year (about 30–45 cars per day) during the 3-month season (see chart on page 103). The yard, like C&NW's Wood Street Yard, included driveways between tracks for truck access, and some tracks had covered platforms so samples from cars could be displayed.

Auction sales were held in an adjoining building. Following sales, about a third of the cars were unloaded either on site or at nearby Pavonia Avenue Yard, which also had platforms (and was mainly used as a milk transfer yard). The remainder of cars were diversions—they were resealed after the auction and forwarded to final buyers.

Most produce terminals were adjacent to large metro rail yards. As perishable cars arrived in the yard, either in blocks or entire trains, they were re-iced if necessary and then switched to the produce tracks. This was most often done during the evening or night, so cars would be positioned and ready for the next market day.

By late afternoon, empties and diversion cars were switched back out of the produce yard, brought back to the freight yard, and classified in appropriate trains. Diversions were high priority, and empties were a lower priority and would be routed back toward their owners.

The variety of cars that could be seen at these terminals was impressive. Depending upon the season, you would likely find cars from all the major owners—Pacific Fruit Express, Santa Fe, Fruit Growers Express, American Refrigerator Transit, Merchant's Despatch—as well as many cars from smaller owners.

In addition, some perishable terminals served as team tracks for meat packers as well. In photo **16**, the view of New York Central's 30th Street Yard shows reefers from packers Rath, Hormel, Swift, and Wilson, along with produce cars from four owners.

The scale of rail operations at produce terminals dropped from the late 1950s through the 1960s, with some terminals eventually going to all-truck access. An example was Cleveland (Northern Ohio Food Terminal), which as of 1962 still received 12,000 cars of fruits and vegetables each year, but also received 13,000 truckloads as well.

New York car float operations

The New York City area was the largest destination for perishable traffic, and the city's Terminal Market comprised a variety of separate yards and selling areas, most of which were served by car floats. Railroads serving the city had yards along the Hudson River in New Jersey with car float docks. Cars were moved to Manhattan on floats pulled by tugboats. Perishable cars would stay on the floats for unloading, saving considerable space compared to the area that would be needed for a standard yard, **17**.

Trucks load from docks of various commission agencies at the Chicago produce terminal in 1941. *John Vachon, Library of Congress*

Hundreds of refrigerator cars await unloading at the Pittsburgh Produce Terminal in September 1942. Cool weather meant many cars arrived in ventilator service. *Ann Rosener, Library of Congress*

A Chicago & North Western Baldwin switcher begins pulling cars from the "potato yard" in Chicago as an icing truck services a refrigerator car (middle) and buyers finish unloading cars (left) in 1957. *Chicago & North Western*

New York Central's 30th Street Yard served as team tracks for both produce and meat cars. *Jim Shaughnessy*

A banana ship offloads directly to railcars on car floats at a pier in Baltimore, similar to how water operations worked in New York. The floats have platforms between tracks to enable car loading and unloading on water. *Baltimore & Ohio*

Here's an example of how these operations occurred, based on Erie Railroad operations, showing how Erie's Chicago-to-New York perishable Train 98 (described in chapter 6) was handled upon its arrival in New Jersey.

Inbound cars are switched to the railroad's Croxton (N.J.) yard, which had a dedicated area (fruit-holding tracks) for perishables. Refrigerator cars are inspected and re-iced at the yard's 850-foot platform as needed. Meanwhile, consignees have been notified that cars have arrived (they would have already received information about the cars while in transit). Along with cars from Train 98, this can include perishable cars from other connections as well as express refrigerator cars inbound from passenger trains. In peak seasons through the 1950s, this could mean upward of 500 perishable cars a day arriving at Croxton.

Consignees notify the railroad agent each day with a list of cars they want unloaded at the auction terminal in New York City the following day. Not all cars will end up in Manhattan: some cars will have a final diversion, perhaps be sold to a wholesaler, grocery chain, or manufacturer, or head to a cold-storage warehouse. There is also export traffic that heads out from New York.

At cutoff time for the terminal, the railroad agent compiles a list of cars and prepares a float order, which lists cars to be loaded on specific car floats and to which berths the floats are assigned. The Erie then assembles trains of the appropriate cars, moving them 40 or 50 at a time from Croxton to Jersey City's float bridge yard on the Hudson, where floats have been placed.

Each car float carries 10–16 cars. The floats are hauled by tugboat across the Hudson River—in the Erie's case to the Duane Street Station in New York City—overnight, usually starting at 8 p.m.

Railroads leased piers from the City of New York's Harbor Department. Piers 20 and 21 were leased by the Erie and were equipped strictly for handling perishables. Each pier was

1,000 feet long with 12 total berths. Four additional floats could be placed outboard of the 12 floats at the berth. This gave Erie the capacity to dock 160 cars at one time. The piers were steam-heated, which kept the temperatures in the low 40s even in the winter.

Cars are unloaded overnight, **18**. While on their floats, the cars are unloaded a float at a time by a gang of workers supervised by a foreman, **19**. Pier space is assigned to consignees, and their allocated areas are chalked on the pier so workers know where to place their goods.

If traffic volume is heavy, floats of empty cars will be pulled away and new floats of loads docked in their place. An Erie publication in 1945 stated that the railroad's record was 367 cars unloaded at Duane Street in a single day.

Cars would all be unloaded and floats removed by early morning. Buyers inspect the produce on display first thing in the morning before the start of auctions at 8 or 8:30 a.m. Once sales have been made, buyers promptly load their goods aboard trucks and wagons for transport throughout the city.

New York railroads were dependent upon these float operations. The Erie in the 1940s, for example, had an extensive water-borne fleet including 12 tugboats and 30 car floats, **20**. By the 1960s, much of this traffic shifted to trucks.

Damage claims

Dealing with damage claims was an issue for shippers, railroads, and buyers, especially at large-volume locations such as produce terminals. Cars would be inspected upon arrival, with inspectors checking condition of the perishables, their packing, and temperature. Depending upon the location, era, and jurisdiction, local health inspectors or U.S. Department of Agriculture inspectors would be on hand, **21**.

The Railroad Perishable Inspection Agency (RPIA)—employed by carriers to provide an independent check of conditions of lading—was formed in 1933. Railroads used this service to mediate consignees claims. A railroad's

Car floats with center platforms allowed reefers to be unloaded while still on the floats. Unloading at piers was done overnight. This is Pier 29 on the Pennsy in 1939.
Arthur Rothstein, Library of Congress

Workers unload cases of Florida celery at New York. The wood strips at lower left had been tacked to the cases to keep them in position during transit.
Arthur Rothstein, Library of Congress

A boxcab diesel pulls cars from a center-platform (station) car float at Erie's Harlem River freight station in 1940. Similar facilities were used to serve other piers and yards in New York. *Erie Railroad*

Inspectors checked inbound loads, making sure cases and products were in good condition and at proper temperatures. *Chicago & North Western*

refusal to pay a claim could be approved or declined by RPIA.

Perishables represented a large portion of railroads' claims—often around 10 percent of revenues and sometimes higher. (One year, Pennsy reported 17 percent of claims on perishable revenues.) Generally, this was a mix of spoilage and damaged crates.

Spoilage was often localized (a few crates from a car), but occasionally an entire car could be condemned. Spoilage could be caused by problems with the car, such as a broken door, bad door seals, broken air-circulating fans, an improperly latched door, damaged sheathing or insulation, or a failed engine or compressor (on a mechanical car).

Spoilage can also be caused by insufficient icing or improper ventilation or heating. Because of this, railroads kept careful records of icing and protective services. For example, if a shipment arrived spoiled but the shipper had ordered limited icing instead of standard icing, the railroad would likely deny the claim.

Broken crates and boxes could also ruin produce. This is why proper packing (see chapter 5) was so important. Undoubtedly shippers would claim rough handling on the part of the railroad, while railroads would contend that shippers didn't pack cases properly (the railroad more often than not would be stuck with the damage claim).

The transition from wood cases to fiberboard and cardboard boxes in the 1940s and '50s caused problems, as the new boxes weren't as strong as crates. Also, unlike wood, the new boxes lost strength as they absorbed moisture, which sometimes led to boxes at the bottom of stacks being crushed en route.

Large terminals would have coopers on hand to repair broken crates. It was often possible to fix minor damage or combine cases and salvage some goods. If some were beyond repair or if the cases were refused by a consignee, the railroad might sell non-spoiled goods at a separate auction or simply write off the damaged products.

Bibliography

Periodicals

"AC&F NWX 40-foot Wood Refrigerator Cars," by Pat Wider, *Railway Prototype Cyclopedia*, Vol. 4, p. 52

"AC&F's URTCo. and MRX Refrigerator Cars, Built May 1927-1929," by Ed Hawkins, *Railway Prototype Cyclopedia*, Vol. 5, p. 42

"Aluminum Reefer Stands Test of Time," *Railway Age*, February 23, 1953

"America's New Refrigerator Cars," by David G. Casdorph, *Freight Cars Journal*, No. 54, p. 1

"American Car & Foundry's 1920s Wood Refrigerator Cars," by Ted Culotta, *Railroad Model Craftsman*, April 2006, p. 93

"American Refrigerator Transit Early Steel Refrigerator Cars," by Richard H. Hendrickson, *RailModel Journal*, June 2007, p. 49

"American Refrigerator Transit Co. 1950s Era Painting Variations," by Charlie Duckworth, *Wabash Railroad Historical Society Banner*, Winter 1996, p. 4

"ART Gets 500 New Reefers," *Railway Age*, December 1, 1952, p. 93

"Banana Road Today," by Terry McMahon, *Green Diamond* (Illinois Central Historical Society), December 2013, p. 4

"Banana Traffic on the Illinois Central," by Terry McMahon, *Green Diamond* (Illinois Central Historical Society), April 1997, p. 4

"Bangor & Aroostook Mechanical Reefers," by George Melvin, *Model Railroading*, February 1991, p. 16

"BR and BS Express Refrigerator Cars," by Pat Wider, *Railway Prototype Cyclopedia*, Vol. 7, p. 1

"Canadian Railways' Refrigerator Cars," by A. N. Campbell, *Railway Age*, June 17, 1950, p. 45

"Case History of a Spud Train," by David P. Morgan, *Great Trains Freight* (Kalmbach), Holiday 2017

"Cotton Belt Speed and Performance Teamed for Better Service," *Railway Age*, June 2, 1952, p. 77

"Cryogenic Cars," by Thornton Waite, *Mainline Modeler*, August 2000, p. 26

"Door Unit Cools Fresh-Produce Car," *Railway Age*, February 12, 1962

"Economy in Operation with Mechanically Cooled Refrigerator Cars," *Railway Age*, October 29, 1951, p. 35

"Express Reefers: De Facto Standard?" by John Nehrich, *Mainline Modeler*, April 1989, p. 54

"Fan Circulation Improves Effectiveness of Refrigerator Cars," by E. A. Gorman, Jr., *Railway Age*, March 30, 1935, p. 493

"FGE's Modern Mechanical Reefers," by David G. Casdorph, *Model Railroading*, November 1997, p. 50

"Field of Dreams," by Elrond Lawrence, *Trains*, December 2004, p. 32

"50-foot FGE Plug-Door Insulated Boxcars," by James Eager, *RailModel Journal*, February 1993, p. 42

"57-foot RPL-Class Reefers From Con-Cor Kits in HO or N Scale," by James Eager, *RailModel Journal*, March 1993, p. 35

"Freight Cars—Repair, Rebuild, or Buy New?" by William Wyer, *Railway Age*, February 4, 1950, p. 38

"Fresh From the West," by Rob Leachman, *The Streamliner* (Union Pacific Historical Society), Spring 2012, p. 6

"Fresh Fruit Every Day," by C. W. Workman, *Trains*, December 1942, p. 26

"GATX Arcticar," by Mark W. Heinz, *Mainline Modeler*, September 1992, p. 25

"General American 70-ton All-Steel Refrigerator Cars," by Patrick C. Wider, *Railway Prototype Cyclopedia*, Vol. 16, p. 54

"Got Carrots?" by Bill Stephens, *Trains*, November 2001, p. 78

"Great Northern Apple Rush," by Charles W. Moore, *Trains*, January 1941, p. 35

"Handling Perishable Traffic," by P. J. Napoli, *Erie Railroad Magazine*, June 1944, p. 8

"History of ART Refrigerator Cars," by Gene Semon, *Model Railroading*, October 1988 (Part 1), March 1989, p. 50 (Part 2), April 1989, p. 53 (Part 3)

"Hot Water Speeds De-icing of Reefers," *Railway Age*, February 4, 1950, p. 48

"How Users View Refrigerator Car Trends," *Railway Age*, February 18, 1952, p. 41

"I Was a Teenage Iceman," by L. Graham "Gray" Dales, *Workin' on the Railroad*, *Classic Trains* special issue, 2011, p. 102

"Icing Facilities of the Pennsylvania Railroad," by Charles H. Geletzke, Jr., *The Keystone* (Pennsylvania Railroad Technical & Historical Society), Summer 1992, p. 44

"Improved Refrigerator Car Design Long Overdue," by Harvey B. Lindsay, *Railway Age*, May 18, 1935, p. 769

"Juice Train!" by Scott A. Hartley, *Trains*, March 2000, p. 36

"The Log of Fruit Block 344," by W. H. Hutchinson, *Trains*, August 1952, p. 54

"The Lost Art of Stage Icing," by Bob Gregson, *Great Northern Historical Society Goat*, June 1982, p. 4 (Part 1), December 1982, p. 4 (Part 2), March 1983, p. 4 (Part 3)

"Mass-Production Icing on Union Pacific," *Railway Age*, June 21, 1947, p. 1250

"MD-22, Georgia Peach Train," by Charles H. Geletzke, Jr., *The Keystone* (Pennsylvania Railroad Technical & Historical Society), Autumn 2001, p. 70

"MDT Refrigerator Cars," by Roger C. Hinman, *Central Headlight* (New York Central Historical Society), 2nd Quarter 1998, p. 13

"Mechanical Controls are Precise," *Railway Age*, April 18, 1955, p. 56

"Mechanical Cooling Pays Its Way," by C. B. Peck, *Railway Age*, April 18, 1955

"Mechanical Reefers: Car of the Future?" Modern Railroads, September 1953, p. 69

"Mechanical Reefers—Or Trailers?" *Modern Railroads*, December 1961, p. 58

"Mechanical Refrigeration of Cars," *Railway Age*, December 23, 1950, p. 27

"Mechanical Refrigeration Package," *Modern Railroads*, March 1951, p. 135

"Mechanization Results in Less Icing Time at Laramie," *Railway Age*, Sept. 12, 1955, p. 49

"Modeling American Refrigerator Transit's 40- and 42-foot Wooden Reefers," by Al Westerfield, *RailModel Journal*, March 1992, p. 12

"NACC Smoothside RBL," by James Kinkaid, *Mainline Modeler*, July 1994, p. 40

"New Patterns in Refrigerated Transport," by Charles W. Donnelly, *Modern Railroads*, December 1961, p. 53

"Northern Pacific's Mechanical Reefers," by Jim Sandrin, *The Mainstreeter* (Northern Pacific Railroad Historical Association), Vol. 12, No. 2, p. 5

"No. 62 Sets Freight Record," (Santa Fe) *Modern Railroads*, July 1953, p. 57

"Operation 'Spuds'—Santa Fe Style," *Modern Railroads*, July 1953, p. 51

"Pacific Fruit Express Builds 2,000 Refrigerator Cars" (R-40-26), *Railway Age*, January 28, 1952, p. 29

"Perishable Demands are Exacting," *Railway Age*, April 18, 1955, p. 53

"Perishable Fruit Traffic on the Northern Pacific," *The Mainstreeter* (Northern Pacific Railroad Historical Association), Vol. 4, No. 2,

"Perishables in All Seasons," *Modern Railroads*, December 1953, p. 63

"Perishables…Priority Traffic," *North Western Lines* (Chicago & North Western Historical Society), Spring 1984, p. 24

"PFE Challenges the Future to the Tune of $237 Million, *Railway Age*, January 30, 1967, p. 33

"PFE is Expanding its Reefer Fleet" (R-70-12), *Railway Age*, July 11, 1960, p. 22

"PFE Received Refrigerator Cars" (R-40-23), *Railway Age*, June 14, 1947, p. 1208

"The Post-War Refrigerator Car," *Railway Age*, January 29, 1949, p. 18

"Perishable Handling—A Mighty Transportation Spectacle," *Railway Age*, December 28, 1935, p. 854

"Perishable Service…It's Fast!" *Modern Railroads*, May 1954, p. 63

"Perishables: Off-beat Problems," *Railway Age*, March 29, 1965, p. 55

"Pittsburgh Produce Terminal," by William G. Dorwart, *The Keystone* (Pennsylvania Railroad Technical & Historical Society), Spring 1990, p. 33

"Problems With Perishables," *Railway Age*, March 30, 1964, p. 50

"Push a Button, Ice a Reefer," *Modern Railroads*, June 1953, p. 101

"The PRR's Tomato Cars," by Charles Blardone, Jr., *The Keystone* (Pennsylvania Railroad Technical & Historical Society), Summer 1984, p. 41

"Quick Handling for Perishables," *Railway Age*, September 27, 1954, p. 43

"Reefers," *Burlington Route Historical Society Bulletin*, No. 12 (second quarter 1984)

"Reefers: A Short History of Refrigerator Cars in America 1840-1984," by William K. Viekman, *Freight Cars Journal*, No. 44, p. 4

"Reefers are a Desert Mirage," by Steve Patterson, *CTC Board*, April 1990, p. 24

"Reefers of the Union Refrigerator Transit Co.," by Al Westerfield, *RailModel Journal*, July 1992, p. 8

"Santa Fe Installs New Car Icing Machine," *Railway Age*, Oct. 17, 1960, p. 28

"Santa Fe Rr-30 Class 50-foot Refrigerator," by Richard Hendrickson, *RailModel Journal*, September 2006, p. 18

"Santa Fe's Rebuilt USRA Reefers," by Ted Culotta, *Railroad Model Craftsman*, August 2006, p. 92

"The SFRD Story: 104 Years of Yellow and Black Reefers," by A. Dean Hale, *Santa Fe Modeler*, 1988? [check], p. 5 (Part 1) and Second Quarter 1989 (Part 2), p. 5

"Shipping California Citrus," by Keith Jordan, *How To Build Realistic Layouts 2007* (Kalmbach), p. 66

"Squeeze in a Juice Distribution Center," by Peter A. Werner, *Model Railroader*, May 2007, p. 70

"They're Built to Maintain Zero," *Railway Age*, April 25, 1955, p. 56

"TOFC Traffic Rises Sharply," *Railway Age*, April 9, 1962, p. 30

"200-Car Ice Dock Straddles New Yard," *Modern Railroads*, October 1954, p. 93

"Two-Way Piggyback Puts Profit in Perishables," by Nancy Ford, *Modern Railroads*, September 1962, p. 110

"Walthers HO & N Scale 76-foot Cryogenic Reefers," by Scott Chatfield, *RailModel Journal*, March 1994, p. 5

"War Babies—The 1940s Wood-Sheathed Cars of the FGE/WFE/BRE Companies," by Bill Welch et. al., *Railway Prototype Cyclopedia*, Vol. 12, p. 88

"Western Fruit Express Refrigerator Cars," by Clive Carter, *Mainline Modeler*, April 1996, p. 41 (Part 1) and May 1996, p. 72 (Part 2)

"What's New About This Car?" (Northern Pacific mechanical reefer), *Railway Age*, December 23, 1957, p. 26

Books

Billboard Refrigerator Cars, by Richard H. Hendrickson and Edward S. Kaminski, Signature Press, 2008

Freight Cars of the '40s and '50s, by Jeff Wilson, Kalmbach Publishing Co., 2015

The Great Yellow Fleet, by John H. White, Golden West Books, 1986

Mechanical Refrigerator Cars and Insulated Refrigerator Cars of the Santa Fe Railway 1948-1988, Santa Fe Rolling Stock Reference Series Vol. 6, by John B. Moore, Jr., Santa Fe Modelers Organization, 2007

Merchants Despatch: Its History and Equipment, by Roger C. Hinman, Signature Press, 2011

The Model Railroader's Guide to Freight Cars, by Jeff Wilson, Kalmbach Publishing Co., 2005

Pacific Fruit Express, Second Edition, by Anthony W. Thompson, Robert J. Church, and Bruce H. Jones, Signature Press, 2000

Refrigerator Car Color Guide, by Gene Green, Morning Sun Books, 2005

Refrigerator Cars: Ice Bunker Cars 1884-1979, Santa Fe Rolling Stock Reference Series Vol. 2, by C. Keith Jordan et. al., Santa Fe Modelers Organization, 1994

Miscellaneous

"Body Icing in Transit Refrigeration of Vegetables," *U.S. Department of Agriculture Technical Bulletin No. 627*, August 1938

Car Builders' Cyclopedia and *Car and Locomotive Cyclopedia*, various editions

Code of Rules for Handling Perishable Freight, Circular No. 20-B, National Perishable Freight Committee, December 15, 1941; and Circular 20-D, September 11, 1958

Erie Railroad Company Instructions Covering Consist and Classification of Scheduled Freight Trains, Office of Superintendent of Transportation, Cleveland, 1950

The Freight Traffic Red Book, 1955 edition, Traffic Publishing Co., New York City

Fruit and Vegetable Loading from Territory Served by Missouri Pacific Lines in Texas, Season 1947-1948, Missouri Pacific Office of Senior Executive Assistant, Houston

"Made to Last: The Santa Fe's USRA Refrigerator Cars," by Keith Jordan, Railroad Prototype Modelers seminar, Naperville, Ill., 2004

Official Railway Equipment Register, various issues

Railway Engineering & Maintenance Cyclopedia, 1948 edition

"Steel Reefers of the FGE/WFE/BRE Fleets: 1937-1955," by Bill Welch, Railroad Prototype Modelers seminar, Naperville, Ill., 2005

Service Instructions for Perishable Freight, Perishable Freight Department, Western Pacific, 1949

"Stage Icing in the Refrigeration of Oranges in Transit from California," *U.S. Department of Agriculture Technical Bulletin No. 857*, September 1943

"The Wood-Sheathed Cars of the FGE/WFEX/BREX Freight Refrigerator Fleet," by Bill Welch, Railroad Prototype Modelers seminar, Naperville, Ill., 2002

About the author

Jeff Wilson has written more than 30 books on railroads and model railroading. He spent 10 years as an associate editor at *Model Railroader* magazine, and he currently works as a freelance writer, editor, and photographer, contributing articles to MR and other magazines. He enjoys many facets of the hobby, especially building structures, as well as photographing both real and model railroads.

Acknowledgments

My profound thanks and appreciation goes to several people who provided photographs and other information: Cody Grivno, Dave Ingles, Keith Kohlmann, and Rob McGonigal. Thanks also to the many photographers whose works reside in the David P. Morgan Library at Kalmbach Publishing Co., without which this book would not have been possible.

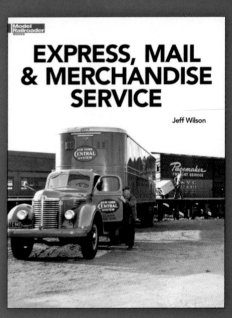